Teach Yourself
VISUALLY™

Adobe® Photoshop®
Elements

by Mike Wooldridge

Visual™

From
maranGraphics®

&

Hungry Minds™

Best-Selling Books • Digital Downloads • e-Books • Answer Networks
e-Newsletters • Branded Web Sites • e-Learning

New York, NY • Cleveland, OH • Indianapolis, IN

Teach Yourself VISUALLY™ Adobe® Photoshop® Elements

Published by
Hungry Minds, Inc.
909 Third Avenue
New York, NY 10022

maranGraphics, Inc.
5755 Coopers Avenue
Mississauga, Ontario, Canada
L4Z 1R9

Library of Congress Control Number: 2002100179

ISBN: 0-7645-3678-8

Printed in the United States of America

10 9 8 7 6 5 4 3 2 1

1K/SU/QU/QS/IN

Distributed in the United States by Hungry Minds, Inc.

Distributed by CDG Books Canada Inc. for Canada; by Transworld Publishers Limited in the United Kingdom; by IDG Norge Books for Norway; by IDG Sweden Books for Sweden; by IDG Books Australia Publishing Corporation Pty. Ltd. for Australia and New Zealand; by TransQuest Publishers Pte Ltd. for Singapore, Malaysia, Thailand, Indonesia, and Hong Kong; by Gotop Information Inc. for Taiwan; by ICG Muse, Inc. for Japan; by Intersoft for South Africa; by Eyrolles for France; by International Thomson Publishing for Germany, Austria and Switzerland; by Distribuidora Cuspide for Argentina; by LR International for Brazil; by Galileo Libros for Chile; by Ediciones ZETA S.C.R. Ltda. for Peru; by WS Computer Publishing Corporation, Inc., for the Philippines; by Contemporanea de Ediciones for Venezuela; by Express Computer Distributors for the Caribbean and West Indies; by Micronesia Media Distributor, Inc. for Micronesia; by Chips Computadoras S.A. de C.V. for Mexico; by Editorial Norma de Panama S.A. for Panama; by American Bookshops for Finland.

For corporate orders, please call maranGraphics at 800-469-6616 or fax 905-890-9434.

For general information on Hungry Minds' products and services please contact our Customer Care Department within the U.S. at 800-762-2974, outside the U.S. at 317-572-3993 or fax 317-572-4002.

For sales inquiries and reseller information, including discounts, premium and bulk quantity sales, and foreign-language translations, please contact our Customer Care Department at 800-434-3422, fax 317-572-4002, or write to Hungry Minds, Inc., Attn: Customer Care Department, 10475 Crosspoint Boulevard, Indianapolis, IN 46256.

For information on licensing foreign or domestic rights, please contact our Sub-Rights Customer Care Department at 212-884-5000.

For information on using Hungry Minds' products and services in the classroom or for ordering examination copies, please contact our Educational Sales Department at 800-434-2086 or fax 317-572-4005.

For press review copies, author interviews, or other publicity information, please contact our Public Relations department at 317-572-3168 or fax 317-572-4168.

For authorization to photocopy items for corporate, personal, or educational use, please contact Copyright Clearance Center, 222 Rosewood Drive, Danvers, MA 01923, or fax 978-750-4470.

Screen shots displayed in this book are based on pre-released software and are subject to change.

Trademark Acknowledgments

Permissions

Hungry Minds™ is a trademark of Hungry Minds, Inc.

U.S. Corporate Sales	**U.S. Trade Sales**
Contact maranGraphics at (800) 469-6616 or Fax (905) 890-9434.	Contact Hungry Minds at (800) 434-3422 or fax (317) 572-4002.

Some comments from our readers...

"I have to praise you and your company on the fine products you turn out. I have twelve of the *Teach Yourself VISUALLY* and *Simplified* books in my house. They were instrumental in helping me pass a difficult computer course. Thank you for creating books that are easy to follow."

   –*Gordon Justin (Brielle, NJ)*

"I commend your efforts and your success. I teach in an outreach program for the Dr. Eugene Clark Library in Lockhart, TX. Your *Teach Yourself VISUALLY* books are incredible and I use them in my computer classes. All my students love them!"

   –*Michele Schalin (Lockhart, TX)*

"Thank you so much for helping people like me learn about computers. The Maran family is just what the doctor ordered. Thank you, thank you, thank you."

   –*Carol Moten (New Kensington, PA)*

"I would like to take this time to compliment maranGraphics on creating such great books. Thank you for making it clear. Keep up the good work."

   –*Kirk Santoro (Burbank, CA)*

"I write to extend my thanks and appreciation for your books. They are clear, easy to follow, and straight to the point. Keep up the good work!

   –*Seward Kollie (Dakar, Senegal)*

"What fantastic teaching books you have produced! Congratulations to you and your staff. You deserve the Nobel prize in Education in the Software category. Thanks for helping me to understand computers."

   –*Bruno Tonon (Melbourne, Australia)*

"Over time, I have bought a number of your 'Read Less – Learn More' books. For me, they are THE way to learn anything easily."

   –*José A. Mazón (Cuba, NY)*

"I was introduced to maranGraphics about four years ago and YOU ARE THE GREATEST THING THAT EVER HAPPENED TO INTRODUCTORY COMPUTER BOOKS!"

   –*Glenn Nettleton (Huntsville, AL)*

"Compliments To The Chef!! Your books are extraordinary! Or, simply put, Extra-Ordinary, meaning way above the rest! THANK YOU THANK YOU THANK YOU! for creating these.

   –*Christine J. Manfrin (Castle Rock, CO)*

"I'm a grandma who was pushed by an 11-year-old grandson to join the computer age. I found myself hopelessly confused and frustrated until I discovered the Visual series. I'm no expert by any means now, but I'm a lot further along than I would have been otherwise. Thank you!"

   –*Carol Louthain (Logansport, IN)*

"Thank you, thank you, thank you....for making it so easy for me to break into this high-tech world. I now own four of your books. I recommend them to anyone who is a beginner like myself. Now....if you could just do one for programming VCRs, it would make my day!"

   –*Gay O'Donnell (Calgary, Alberta, Canada)*

"You're marvelous! I am greatly in your debt."

   –*Patrick Baird (Lacey, WA)*

**maranGraphics is a family-run business
located near Toronto, Canada.**

At **maranGraphics**, we believe in producing great computer books — one book at a time.

maranGraphics has been producing high-technology products for over 25 years, which enables us to offer the computer book community a unique communication process.

Our computer books use an integrated communication process, which is very different from the approach used in other computer books. Each spread is, in essence, a flow chart — the text and screen shots are totally incorporated into the layout of the spread.

Introductory text and helpful tips complete the learning experience.

maranGraphics' approach encourages the left and right sides of the brain to work together — resulting in faster orientation and greater memory retention.

Above all, we are very proud of the handcrafted nature of our books. Our carefully-chosen writers are experts in their fields, and spend countless hours researching and organizing the content for each topic. Our artists rebuild every screen shot to provide the best clarity possible, making our

screen shots the most precise and easiest to read in the industry. We strive for perfection, and believe that the time spent handcrafting each element results in the best computer books money can buy.

Thank you for purchasing this book. We hope you enjoy it!

Sincerely,

Robert Maran
President
maranGraphics
Rob@maran.com
www.maran.com
www.hungryminds.com/visual

CREDITS

Acquisitions, Editorial, and Media Development

Project Editor
Maureen Spears

Acquisitions Editor
Jen Dorsey

Product Development Supervisor
Lindsay Sandman

Copy Editors
Jerelind Charles, Jill Mazurczyk

Technical Editor
Dennis Cohen

Editorial Manager
Rev Mengle

Permissions Editor
Laura Moss

Editorial Assistant
Amanda Foxworth

Production

Book Design
maranGraphics®

Production Coordinator
Nancee Reeves

Layout
Beth Brooks, Melanie DesJardins, Joyce Haughey,
LeAndra Johnson, Kristin McMullan, Betty Schulte

Screen Artists
Mark Harris, Jill A. Proll

Illustrators
Ronda David-Burroughs, David E. Gregory

Proofreader
Christine Pingleton

Quality Control
John Bitter

Indexer
Sherry Massey

Special Help
Sarah Hellert

ACKNOWLEDGMENTS

General and Administrative

Wiley Technology Publishing Group: Richard Swadley, Vice President & Executive Group Publisher; Bob Ipsen, Vice President & Executive Publisher; Joseph Wikert, Vice President & Publisher; Barry Pruett, Vice President & Publisher; Mary Bednarek, Editorial Director; Andy Cummings, Editorial Director

Wiley Production for Branded Press: Debbie Stailey, Production Director

ABOUT THE AUTHOR

Mike Wooldridge is a technology writer, Web designer, and educator in the San Francisco Bay Area. He is also the author of several other VISUAL books, including *Teach Yourself Visually Illustrator 10*, *Teach Yourself Visually Dreamweaver 4*, *Teach Yourself Visually Photoshop 6*, and *Master Visually Dreamweaver 4 and Flash 5*.

AUTHOR'S ACKNOWLEDGMENTS

Thanks to Maureen Spears, Jennifer Dorsey, Jerelind Charles, Jill Mazurczyk, and the rest of the editorial crew at Hungry Minds. It was great working with everyone again. Also, thanks to Mark Harris, Jill Proll, Ronda David-Burroughs and David Gregory for their hard work on the art for this book. Special thanks to Sarah Hellert and proofreader, Christine Pingleton.

To my two-year old son, Griffin, the subject of
most of our family's photos.

TABLE OF CONTENTS

Chapter 1

Chapter 2

Chapter 3

CHANGING THE SIZE OF AN IMAGE

Chapter 4

MAKING SELECTIONS

Chapter 5

MANIPULATING SELECTIONS

TABLE OF CONTENTS

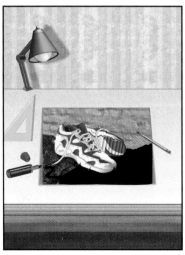

Chapter 8

WORKING WITH LAYERS

Chapter 9

APPLYING EFFECTS AND STYLES

TABLE OF CONTENTS

Chapter 10

APPLYING FILTERS

Chapter 11

ADDING AND MANIPULATING TYPE

Chapter 12

AUTOMATING YOUR WORK

Chapter 13

SAVING FILES

Chapter 14

PRINTING IMAGES

Chapter 15

PERFORMANCE TIPS

HOW TO USE THIS BOOK

Teach Yourself VISUALLY Adobe Photoshop Elements contains straightforward sections, which you can use to learn the basics of Elements. This book is designed to help a reader receive quick access to any area of question. You can simply look up a subject within the Table of Contents or Index and go immediately to the section of concern. A *section* is a set of self-contained units that walk you through a computer operation step-by-step. That is, with rare exception, all the information you need regarding an area of interest is contained within a specific section.

The Organization of Each Chapter

Each task contains an introduction, a set of screen shots, and, if the task goes beyond 1 page, a tip. The introduction tells why you want to perform the task, the advantages and disadvantages of performing the task, and references to other related tasks in the book. The screens, located on the bottom half of each page, show a series of steps that you must complete to perform a given section. The tip portion of the section gives you an opportunity to further understand the task at hand, to learn about other related tasks in other areas of the book, or to apply alternative methods.

A chapter may also contain an illustrated group of pages that gives you background information that you need to understand the sections in a chapter.

The General Organization of This Book

Teach Yourself VISUALLY Adobe Photoshop Elements has 15 chapters. Chapter 1 tells you all about the Elements workspace and how to perform essential commands. Chapter 2 discusses selection tools and how to navigate in Elements. Chapter 3 shows you how resize your image. Chapters 4 and 5 tell you how to select a section of an image so that you can manipulate it to suit your needs. You learn the finer points of coloring your image in Chapters 6 and 7. Chapter 8 shows how to place different objects in your image in layers. You learn about the various effects and filters you can apply to your image in Chapters 9 and 10, while Chapter 11 illustrates how to insert type. Chapters 12 through 15 cover how to save, print and automate your work as well as how to get the most out of Elements with performance tips.

Who This Book Is For

This book is highly recommended for the visual learner who wants to learn the basics of Elements, and who may or may not have prior experience with a computer.

What You Need To Use This Book

To perform the tasks in this book, you need a computer installed with Adobe Photoshop Elements. The system requirements for Elements are listed below. For more information, visit the Adobe Web site at www.adobe.com.

Windows
- Intel® Pentium® class processor.
- Microsoft® Windows® 98, Windows 98 Second Edition, Windows Millennium Edition, Windows 2000, Windows NT® 4.0, or Windows XP.
- Internet Explorer 4.0, 5.0, or 5.5.
- 64 MB of RAM.
- 150 MB of available hard-disk space.
- Color monitor with 256-color (8 bit) or greater video card.
- 800 x 600 or greater monitor resolution.
- CD-ROM drive

Macintosh
- PowerPC® processor.
- Mac OS software version 8.6, 9.0, 9.0.4, or 9.1.
- 64 MB of RAM (with virtual memory on).
- 150 MB of available hard-disk space.
- Color monitor with 256-color (8 bit) or greater video card.
- 800 x 600 or greater monitor resolution.
- CD-ROM drive

Conventions When Using the Mouse

This book uses the following conventions to describe the actions you perform when using the mouse:

Click

Press and release the left mouse button. You use a click to select an item on the screen.

Double-click

Quickly press and release the left mouse button twice. You double-click to open a document or start a program.

Right-click

Press and release the right mouse button. You use a right-click to display a shortcut menu, a list of commands specifically related to the selected item.

Click and Drag, and Release the Mouse

Position the mouse pointer over an item on the screen and then press and hold down the left mouse button. Still holding down the button, move the mouse to where you want to place the item and then release the button. Dragging and dropping makes it easy to move an item to a new location.

The Conventions in This Book

A number of typographic and layout styles have been used throughout Microsoft Office XP to distinguish different types of information.

Bold

Indicates what you must click in a menu or dialog box.

Italics

Indicate a new term being introduced.

Numbered Steps

Indicate that you must perform these steps in order to successfully perform the task.

Bulleted Steps

Give you alternative methods, explain various options, or present what a program will do in response to the numbered steps.

Notes

Give you additional information to help you complete a task. The purpose of a note is threefold: It can explain special conditions that may occur during the course of the task, warn you of potentially dangerous situations, or refer you to tasks in the same, or a different chapter. References to tasks within the chapter are indicated by the phrase "See the section..." followed by the name of the task. References to other chapters are indicated by "See Chapter..." followed by the chapter number.

Icons

Indicate a button that you must click to perform a section.

Conventions That Are Assumed with This Book

Windows and Mac Conventions

Although this book shows you how to perform steps using a PC, you can also perform them on a Mac. When there is a difference between the platforms' keyboards or menu conventions, this book lists the PC convention first, followed by the Mac convention in parentheses. For example:

1 Click **Select**.
2 Click **All**.
■ You can also press `Ctrl` + `A` (`⌘` + `A`) to select all the pixels in an image.

Operating Differences

This book assumes that you have either Windows Me (PC), or OS X (Mac) installed on your computer. Other Windows or OS versions may give different results than those presented in this book.

CHAPTER 1

Getting Started

Are you interested in creating, modifying, combining, and optimizing digital images on your computer? This chapter introduces you to Adobe Photoshop Elements, a popular software application for working with digital images.

Photoshop Elements lets you create, modify, combine, and optimize digital images. You can then save the images to print out or use online.

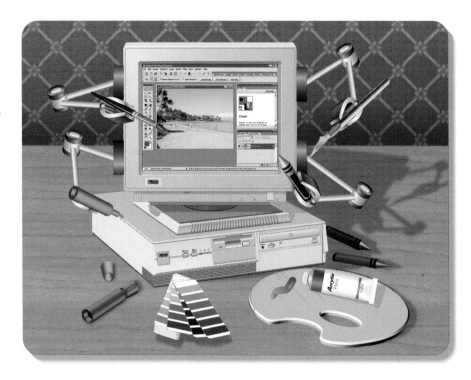

Manipulate Photos

As its name suggests, Photoshop Elements excels at editing digital photographs. You can use the program to make subtle changes, such as to adjust the color in a scanned photo, or you can use its elaborate filters to make your snapshots look like abstract art. See Chapter 7 for more about adjusting color and Chapter 10 for more about filters.

Paint Pictures

Photoshop Elements' painting features make it a formidable illustration tool as well as a photo editor. You can apply colors or patterns to your images with a variety of brush styles. See Chapter 6 for more about applying color. In addition, you can use the application's typographic tools to integrate stylized letters and words into your images. See Chapter 11 for more about type.

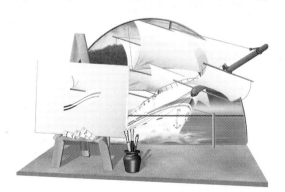

Create a Digital Collage

You can combine different image elements in Photoshop Elements. Your compositions can include photos, scanned art, text, and anything else you can save on your computer as a digital image. By placing elements in Photoshop onto separate layers, you can move, transform, and customize them independently of one another. See Chapter 8 for more about layers.

Organize Your Photos

Photoshop Elements offers useful ways to keep your images organized after you edit them. You can archive your images on contact sheets or display them in a Web photo gallery.

Put Your Images to Work

After you edit your work, you can utilize your images in a variety of ways. Photoshop Elements lets you print your images, save them in a format suitable for placement on a Web page, or prepare them for use in a page-layout program. See Chapter 14 for more about printing. See Chapter 13 for more about using images on the Web.

√

Photoshop Elements' tools let you move, color, stylize, and add text to your images. You can correct color flows in your photographs or turn them into interesting works of art.

Understanding Pixels

Digital images in Photoshop Elements consist of tiny, solid-color squares called *pixels*. Photoshop Elements works its magic by rearranging and re-coloring these squares. If you zoom in close, you can see the pixels that make up your image. To learn how to use the Zoom tool, see Chapter 2.

Choose Your Pixels

To edit specific pixels in your image, you first have to select them by using one of Photoshop Elements' selection tools. See Chapter 4 for more on selection tools. Photoshop also has a number of commands that help you select specific parts of your image, including commands that expand or contract your existing selection or select pixels of a specific color. Chapter 5 covers these commands.

Paint

After selecting your pixels, you can apply color to them by using Photoshop Elements' paintbrush, airbrush, and pencil tools. You can also fill your selections with solid or semitransparent colors. Painting is covered in Chapter 6.

Adjust Color

You can brighten, darken, and change the hue of colors in parts of your image with Photoshop Elements' Dodge, Burn, and similar tools. Other commands display interactive dialog boxes that let you make wholesale color adjustments, letting you precisely correct overly dark or light digital photographs. See Chapter 7 for details.

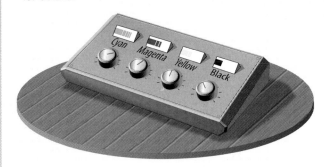

Apply Effects and Filters

Photoshop Elements' effects let you easily add drop shadows, frame borders, and other styles to your images. You can also perform complex color manipulations or distortions by using Photoshop filters. Filters can make your image look like an impressionist painting, apply sharpening or blurring, or distort your image in various ways. Chapters 9 and 10 cover effects and filters.

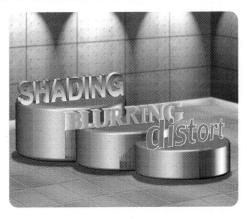

Add Type

Photoshop Elements' type tools enable you to easily apply titles and labels to your images. You can combine these tools with the application's special effects commands to create warped, 3D, or wildly colored type. You can find out more about type in Chapter 11.

You can start Photoshop
Elements on a PC and
begin creating and
editing digital images.

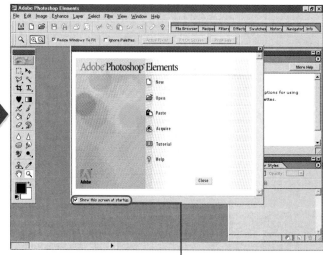

START PHOTOSHOP ELEMENTS ON A PC

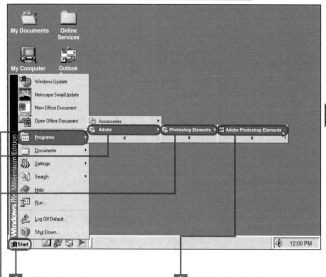

1 Click **Start**.

2 Click **Programs**.

3 Click **Adobe**.

4 Click **Photoshop
Elements**.

5 Click **Adobe Photoshop
Elements**.

*Note: Your path to the Photoshop
Elements application may be
different, depending on how
you installed your software.*

■ Photoshop Elements
starts.

■ A window appears
with clickable shortcuts to
common Elements tasks.

■ You can deselect **Show
this screen at startup** (☑
changes to ☐) to avoid the
window in the future.

START PHOTOSHOP ELEMENTS ON A MAC

You can start Photoshop
Elements on a Macintosh
and begin creating and
editing digital images.

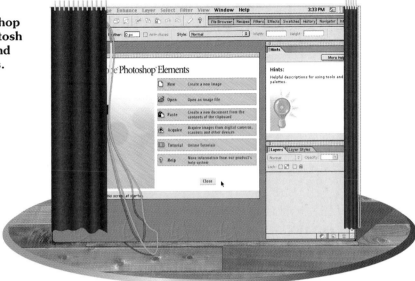

START PHOTOSHOP ELEMENTS ON A MAC

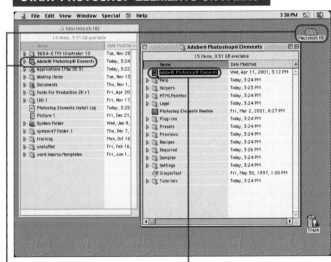

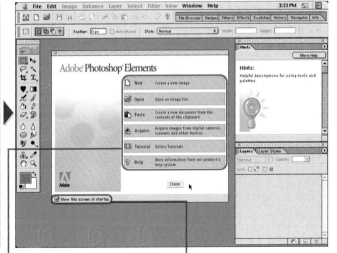

1 Double-click your hard
drive.

2 Double-click the Adobe
Photoshop Elements folder
(📁).

3 Double-click the Adobe
Photoshop Elements icon
(📷).

*Note: The exact location of the
Adobe Photoshop Elements icon
may be different, depending on how
you installed your software and what
version you have.*

■ Photoshop Elements
starts.

■ A window appears
with clickable shortcuts to
common Elements tasks.

■ You can deselect **Show
this screen at startup** (☑
changes to ☐) to avoid the
window in the future.

THE PHOTOSHOP ELEMENTS WORKSPACE

You can use a combination of tools, menu commands, and palette-based features to open and edit your digital images in Photoshop Elements. For more information about palettes, see the section "Open and Close Palettes."

Shortcuts Bar

Displays clickable icons for common commands.

Palette Well

Stores palettes not currently in use.

Options Bar

Displays controls that let you customize the selected tool in the toolbox.

Elements Toolbox

Displays a variety of icons, each one representing an image-editing tool. You click and drag inside your image to apply most of the tools.

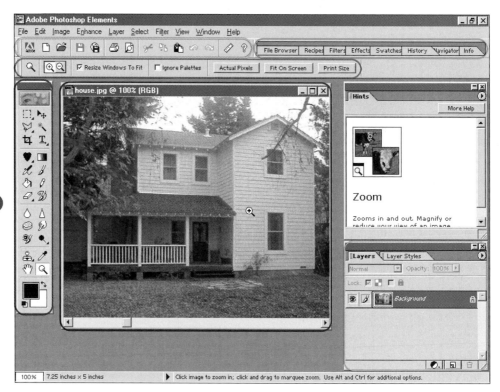

Image Window

Contains each image you open in Elements.

Palettes

Small, free-floating windows that give you access to common commands and resources.

FIND IMAGES FOR YOUR PROJECTS

You can get raw material for using Photoshop Elements from a variety of sources.

Start from Scratch

You can create your Photoshop Elements image from scratch by opening a blank canvas in an image window. Then you can apply color and patterns with Photoshop's painting tools or cut and paste parts of other images to create a composite. See the section "Create a New Image" in this chapter for more on opening a blank canvas.

Scanned Photos and Art

A scanner gives you an inexpensive way to convert existing paper-based content into digital form. You can scan photos and art into your computer, retouch and stylize them in Photoshop Elements, and then output them to a color printer.

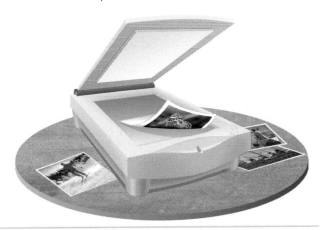

Clip Art

If you want a wide variety of image content with which to work, consider buying a clip art collection. Such collections usually include illustrations, photos, and decorative icons that you can use in imaging projects. Most software stores sell clip art; you can also buy downloadable clip art online.

Digital Photos

Digital cameras are a great way to get digital images onto your computer. Most digital cameras save their images in JPEG or TIFF format, both of which you can open and edit in Photoshop Elements. The program's color adjustment tools are great for correcting color and exposure flaws in digital camera images.

OPEN OR CLOSE PALETTES

You can open free-floating windows called *palettes* to access different Elements features. Elements stores closed palettes in the palette well.

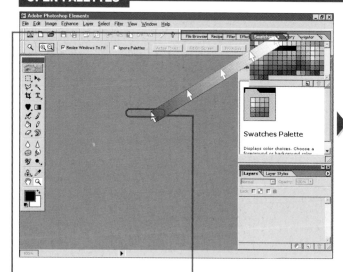

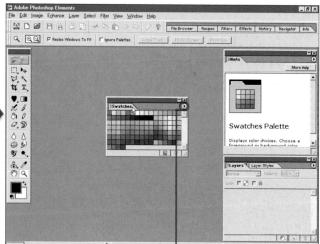

1 Click a tab in the palette well.

■ The palette opens.

2 Click and drag the tab to the work area.

3 Release the mouse.

■ The palette opens as a free-floating window.

■ You can click the palette menu button (⊙) to access commands relevant to the palette.

How do I open several palettes in the same window?

Drag a palette tab to an already open palette window, instead of to the work area. You can switch between multiple palettes in the same window by clicking their tabs.

CLOSE PALETTES

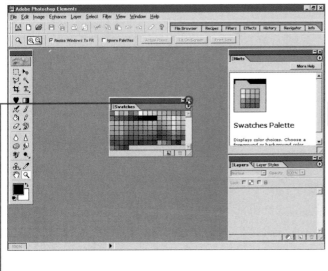

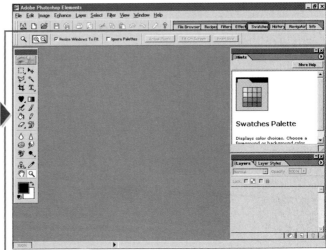

1 Click the close button ⊠ (▣ on the upper-left corner).

■ The palette closes and its tab appears in the palette well.

SET PREFERENCES

Photoshop Elements'
Preferences dialog boxes
let you change default
settings and customize
how the program looks.

SET PREFERENCES

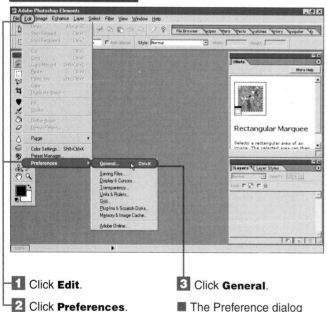

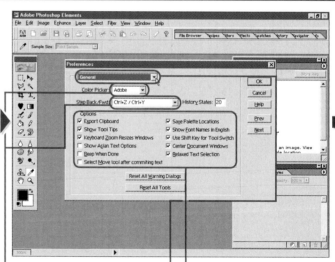

1 Click **Edit**.

2 Click **Preferences**.

3 Click **General**.

■ The Preference dialog
box appears and displays
General options.

4 Click here to determine
which dialog box appears
when you select a color.

5 Click here to select
a keyboard shortcut for
stepping through recent
commands.

6 Click the interface options
you want to use (☐ changes
to ☑).

7 Click ▼ (♦) and select
Display & Cursors.

What type of measurement units should I use in Elements?

Typically, you should use the units most applicable to the type of output you intend to use. Pixel units are useful for Web imaging because monitor dimensions are measured in pixels. Inches or picas are useful for print because those are standards for working on paper.

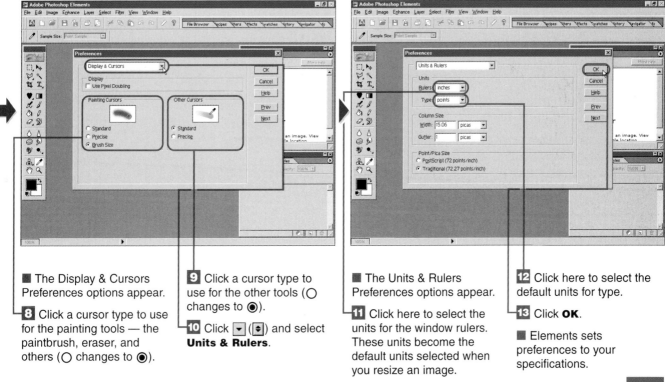

■ The Display & Cursors Preferences options appear.

8 Click a cursor type to use for the painting tools — the paintbrush, eraser, and others (○ changes to ◉).

9 Click a cursor type to use for the other tools (○ changes to ◉).

10 Click ▼ (🖢) and select **Units & Rulers**.

■ The Units & Rulers Preferences options appear.

11 Click here to select the units for the window rulers. These units become the default units selected when you resize an image.

12 Click here to select the default units for type.

13 Click **OK**.

■ Elements sets preferences to your specifications.

GET HELP

Photoshop Elements comes with plenty of electronic documentation that you can access in case you ever need help.

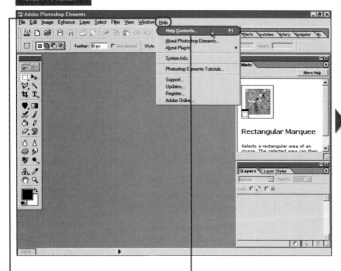

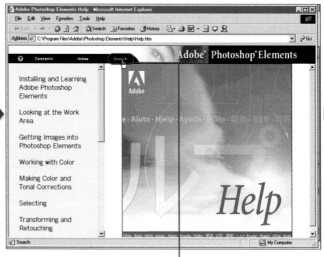

1 Click **Help**.

2 Click **Help Contents**.

■ Elements opens a Web browser and displays the Help interface.

3 Click **Search** to search for information about a particular topic.

How can I get additional tips and news about Photoshop?

Click **Help** and then **Adobe Online** to access information about product support, software upgrades, and third-party add-ons for Photoshop Elements at the Adobe Web site. You need an Internet connection to get information via Adobe Online.

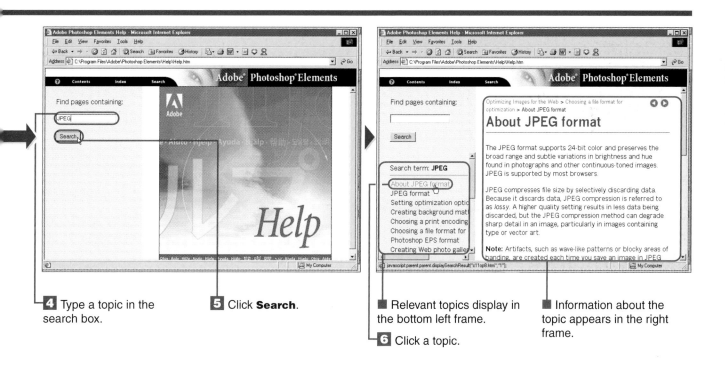

4 Type a topic in the search box.

5 Click **Search**.

■ Relevant topics display in the bottom left frame.

6 Click a topic.

■ Information about the topic appears in the right frame.

VIEW HINTS

The Hints palette briefly explains how to use the currently selected tool or palette. Hints are useful if you want to quickly know how a feature in Elements works.

VIEW HINTS

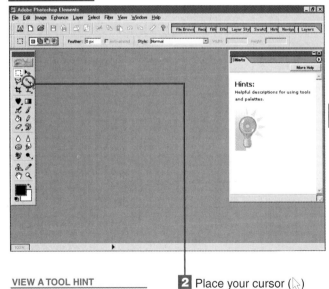

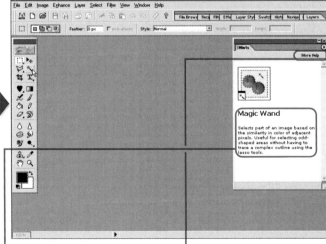

VIEW A TOOL HINT

1 Open the Hints palette.

Note: See the section "Open and Close Palettes" for more information.

2 Place your cursor ( ) over a tool in the toolbox.

■ Information about the tool displays.

■ To view more detailed information, click **More Help** to open the Help documentation.

How can I find details about my Photoshop Elements software?

Click **Help** and then **System Info.** A window opens displaying information about your Elements software, including where it is installed and what plug-ins you have available. It also lists basic information about your computer's operating system and memory.

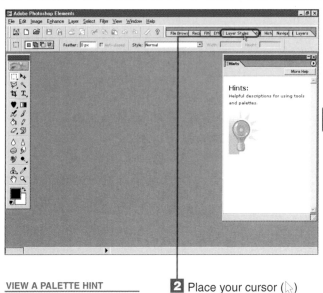

VIEW A PALETTE HINT

1 Open the Hints palette.

Note: See the section "Open and Close Palettes" for more information.

2 Place your cursor ( ) over a palette tab.

■ Information about the palette displays.

■ To view more detailed information, click **More Help** to open the Help documentation.

USING A RECIPE

The Recipes palette displays step-by-step instructions for performing common image-editing tasks. Recipes can help you become accustomed to using Photoshop Elements.

Open Image:
1. Click File.
2. Click Open.
3. Choose File.
4. Click Open.

USING A RECIPE

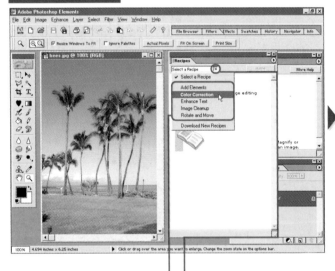

1 Open the Recipes palette.

Note: See the section "Open and Close Palettes" for more information.

2 Click ▼ (◆).

3 Click a recipe category.

■ A listing of topics for that category displays.

4 Click a recipe topic.

Are there recipes for correcting color problems or flaws in my digital photos?

Photoshop Elements includes a number of recipes for fixing digital photos. Open the Recipes palette and then select the **Color Correction** or **Image Cleanup** categories to access these recipes. Some of the topics include removing a color cast and getting rid of dust and scratches.

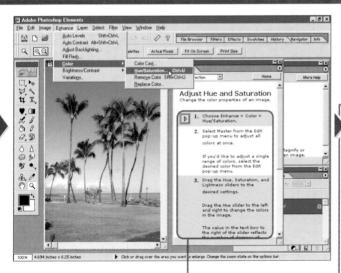

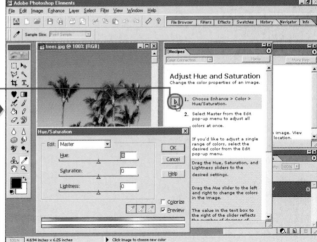

■ The Recipe palette displays the steps required to complete the topic.

5 Complete each step in the recipe.

■ A play button (▶) indicates that Photoshop Elements can complete the step automatically.

6 Click ▶ to have Elements complete a step.

■ Elements completes the step for you.

■ In this example, Elements opens the Hue/Saturation dialog box.

OPEN AN IMAGE

You can open an existing image file in Photoshop Elements to modify it or use it in a project.

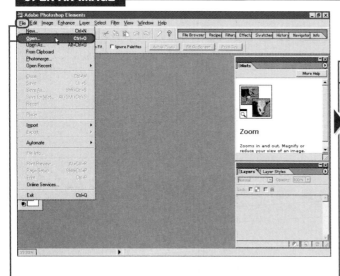

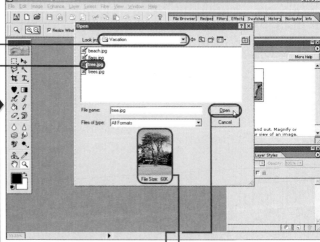

OPEN AN EXISTING IMAGE

1 Click **File**.

2 Click **Open**.

■ You can also click the Folder icon (📁) in the Shortcuts bar to open the file.

■ The Open dialog box appears.

3 Click ▼ (🔽) to browse to the folder that contains the image you want to open.

4 Click the filename of the image you want to open.

■ A preview of the image displays. On a Mac, you can click Show Preview to display a preview.

5 Click **Open**.

What types of files can Photoshop Elements open?

Photoshop Elements can open most of the image file formats in common use today. Here are a few of the more popular ones:

BMP (Bitmap)	The standard Windows image format
PICT	The standard Macintosh image format
TIFF (Tagged Image File Format)	A popular format for print on Windows and Macintosh
EPS (Encapsulated PostScript)	Another print-oriented format
JPEG (Joint Photographic Experts Group)	A format for Web images
GIF (Graphics Interchange Format)	Another format for Web images
PSD (Photoshop Document)	Photoshop's native file format

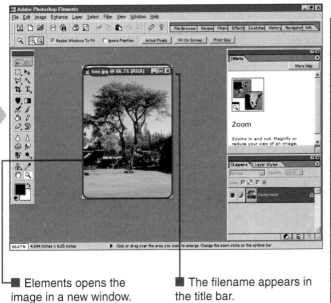

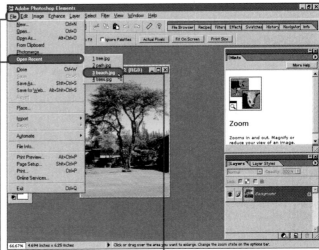

■ Elements opens the image in a new window.

■ The filename appears in the title bar.

OPEN RECENTLY ACCESSED FILES

1 Click **File**.

2 Click **Open Recent**.

■ A list of recently opened files displays.

Note: To specify the number of files that appear in the menu, see the section "Set Preferences."

3 Click the image's filename.

■ Elements opens the image in a new window.

BROWSE FOR AN IMAGE

You can open an existing image file by using Photoshop Elements' File Browser. Browsing offers a user-friendly way to find and open your images.

BROWSE FOR AN IMAGE

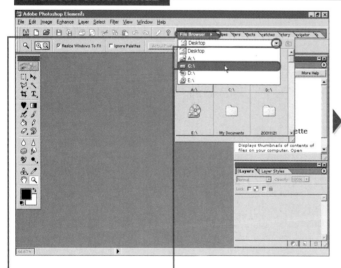

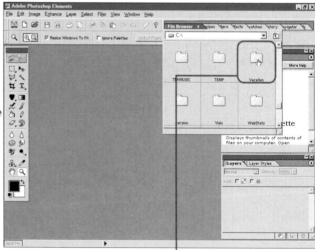

1 Click the **File Browser** tab in the palette well.

*Note: To open the File Browser tab, click **Window** and then **Show File Browser**.*

■ The File Browser opens.

2 Click ▼ (⬍).

3 Click a location on your computer to browse.

■ The folders and files inside the location display.

4 Double-click a folder to open it.

Where should I store my images on my computer?

You may find it helpful to keep all of your images in a single folder somewhere central on your computer, such as on your desktop or inside your My Documents folder, if you have Windows. For Mac OS 9 or later, you can place images in the Documents folder. You may want to create subfolders named with dates or subjects to further organize the images. Keeping images in one place makes it easy to access them from Photoshop Elements.

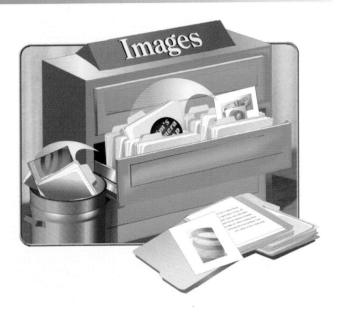

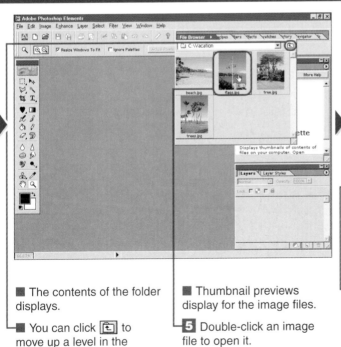

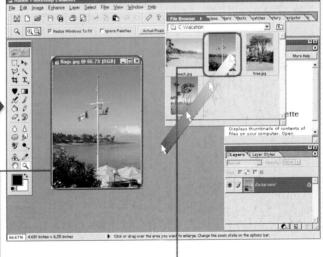

■ The contents of the folder displays.

■ You can click 🔄 to move up a level in the folder hierarchy.

■ Thumbnail previews display for the image files.

5 Double-click an image file to open it.

■ The image opens.

■ You can also click and drag an image file from the File Browser to the work area to open it.

CREATE A NEW IMAGE

You can start a
Photoshop Elements
project by creating
a new blank image.

CREATE A NEW IMAGE

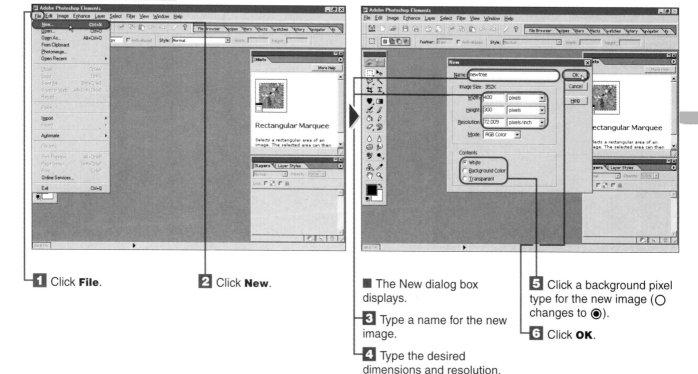

1 Click **File**.

2 Click **New**.

■ The New dialog box
displays.

3 Type a name for the new
image.

4 Type the desired
dimensions and resolution.

5 Click a background pixel
type for the new image (○
changes to ◉).

6 Click **OK**.

How do I choose a resolution for a new image?

The appropriate resolution depends on how you will eventually use the image. For Web or multimedia images, select 72 pixels/inch — the standard resolution for on-screen images. To print black-and-white images on regular paper on a laser printer, 150 pixels/inch probably suffices. For full-color magazine or brochure images, you should use a higher resolution — at least 250 pixels/inch.

72 PIXELS/INCH   150 PIXELS/INCH   250 PIXELS/INCH

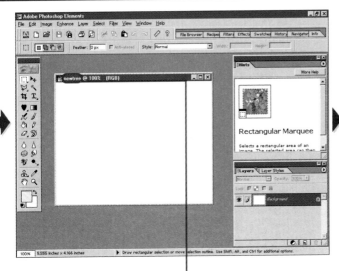

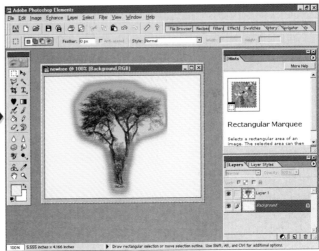

■ Elements creates a new image window at the specified dimensions.

■ The filename appears in the title bar.

7 Use Photoshop's tools and commands to create your image.

■ In this example, part of another image was cut and pasted into the window, and then color was added around it.

Note: To save your image, see the section "Save an Image."

PLACE A FILE

You can place a
file containing
previously
created artwork
into your image.
You can place
several files to
create a digital
collage.

Photoshop
Elements lets
you place
PDF, Adobe
Illustrator, and
EPS files.

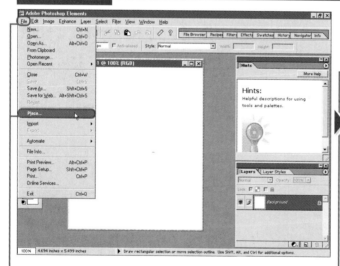

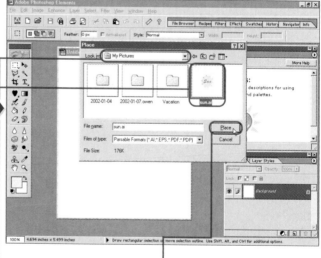

1 Click **File**.

2 Click **Place**.

■ The Place dialog box
appears.

3 Click ▼ (◆) to browse to
the folder that contains the
file you want to open.

4 Click the filename of the
file you want to place.

■ On a Mac, you can click
Show Preview to view a
preview of your images.

5 Click **Place**.

How do I keep proportions constant as I resize my placed artwork?

Click the Maintain Aspect Ratio button () in the Options bar. The proportions will remain constant as you click and drag the corner handles to resize the artwork.

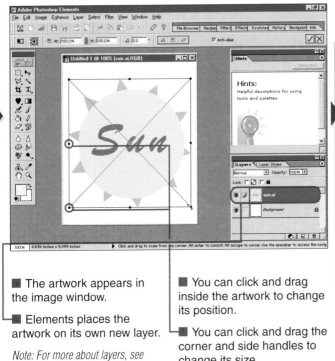

- ■ The artwork appears in the image window.

- ■ Elements places the artwork on its own new layer.

Note: For more about layers, see Chapter 8.

- ■ You can click and drag inside the artwork to change its position.

- ■ You can click and drag the corner and side handles to change its size.

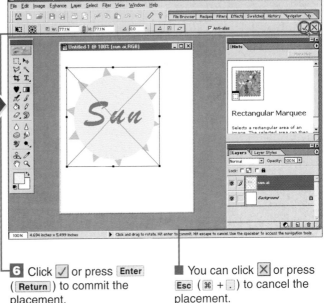

6 Click ✓ or press **Enter** (**Return**) to commit the placement.

- ■ You can click ✕ or press **Esc** (**⌘** + **.**) to cancel the placement.

SAVE AN IMAGE

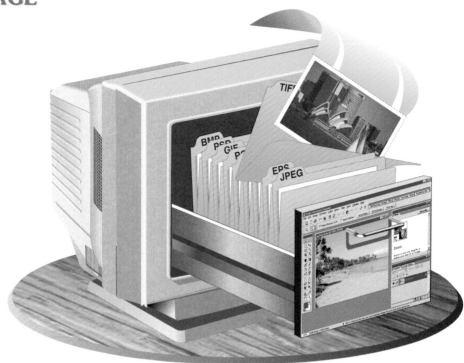

You can save an image in Photoshop Elements to store any changes that you make to it.

Consider saving your images regularly to avoid losing important changes in the event of a system crash.

SAVE AN IMAGE

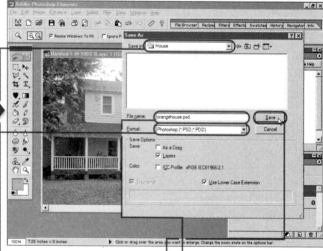

1 Click **File**.

2 Click **Save As**.

■ The Save As dialog box appears.

*Note: For images that you have previously saved, you can click **File** and then **Save**.*

3 Click ▼ (♦) to select a folder to store the file.

4 Click ▼ (♦) to select a file format.

Note: See Chapter 13 for more information on formats.

5 Type a name for the file.

6 Click **Save**.

■ Elements saves the image file.

EXIT PHOTOSHOP ELEMENTS

You can exit
Photoshop
Elements after
you finish using
the application.

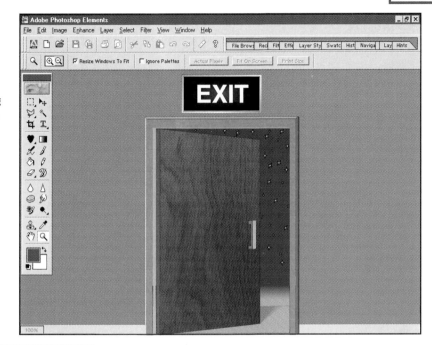

You should always
exit Elements and
all other applications
before shutting down
your computer.

EXIT PHOTOSHOP ELEMENTS

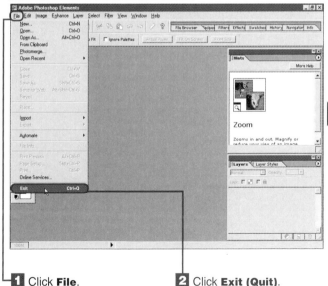

1 Click **File**.

2 Click **Exit (Quit)**.

3 Elements exits.

■ Before exiting, Elements
alerts you to any open images
that have unsaved changes
so you can save them.

*Note: See the section "Save an
Image" to save image files.*

31

CHAPTER 2

Understanding Photoshop Elements Basics

Are you ready to start working with images? This chapter shows you how to select tools and fine-tune your work space.

MAGNIFY WITH THE ZOOM TOOL

You can change the
magnification of an
image with the Zoom
tool. This allows you to
view small details in an
image or view an image
at full size.

MAGNIFY WITH THE ZOOM TOOL

INCREASE MAGNIFICATION

■1 Click the Zoom tool (🔍).

■2 Click the image.

■ Elements increases the
magnification of the image.

■ The point that you clicked
in the image is centered in
the window.

■ The current magnification
shows in the title bar and
status bar.

■ You can choose an exact
magnification by typing a
percentage value in the
status bar.

How do I quickly return an image to 100% magnification?

Double-click  in the toolbox, click **Actual Pixels** on the Options bar, or click **View** and then **Actual Pixels** from the menus.

DECREASE MAGNIFICATION

1 Click the Zoom Out button (🔍).

2 Click the image.

■ Elements decreases the magnification of the image.

■ You can also press and hold **Alt** (**option**) and click the image to decrease magnification.

MAGNIFY A DETAIL

1 Click the Zoom-In button (🔍).

2 Click and drag with the Zoom tool to select the detail.

■ The detail appears enlarged on-screen.

ADJUST VIEWS

You can move an image within the window by using the Hand tool or scroll bars. The Hand tool helps you navigate to an exact area on the image.

The Hand tool is a more flexible alternative to using the scroll bars because, unlike the scroll bars, the Hand tool enables you to drag the image freely in two dimensions.

ADJUST VIEWS

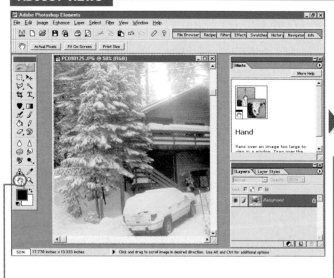

USING THE HAND TOOL

1 Click the Hand tool ( ).

Note: For to produce an effect, the image must be larger than the image window.

2 Click and drag inside the image window.

How can I quickly adjust the image window to see the entire image at its largest possible magnification on-screen?

You have three different ways to magnify the image to its largest possible size: By double-clicking , by clicking the **Fit On Screen** button on the Options bar, or by clicking **View** and then **Fit on Screen** from the menus.

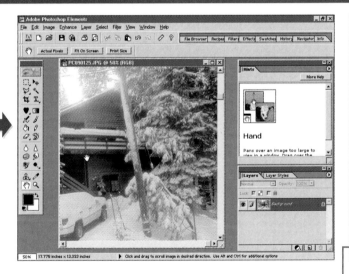

■ The view of the image shifts inside the window.

USING THE SCROLL BARS

1 Click and hold one of the window's scroll bar buttons (◄, ►, ▲, or ▼).

■ The image scrolls.

VIEW RULERS

You can turn on rulers to help you accurately measure and place objects in your image. Rulers let you place objects a specific distance from one another.

You can turn on a grid to place objects with even more precision. See the section "View a Grid" for more information.

VIEW RULERS

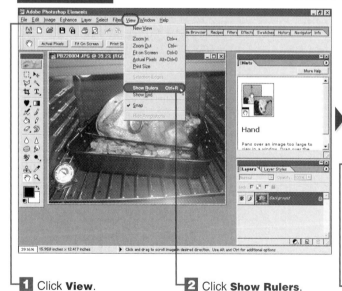

1 Click **View**.

2 Click **Show Rulers**.

■ Photoshop adds rulers to the top and left sides of the image window.

■ To adjust the units of the rulers, click **Edit**, **Preferences**, and then **Units & Rulers**.

VIEW A GRID

You can turn on a grid that overlays your image. A grid can help you precisely organize objects within your image, especially when used with rulers turned on.

See the section "View Rulers" in this chapter for more on rulers.

VIEW A GRID

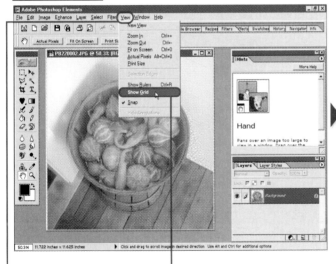

1 Click **View**.

2 Click **Show Grid**.

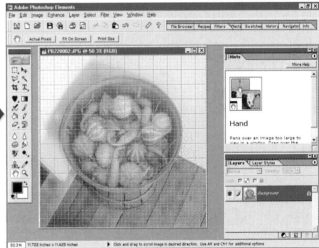

■ A grid appears on top of the image.

■ To adjust the space separating the grid lines, click **Edit**, **Preferences**, and then **Grid**.

■ When you select **View** and then **Snap**, objects in an image align with the grid lines when you move the objects close to them.

USING SHORTCUTS TO SELECT TOOLS

You can press letter keys to select items in the toolbox. You may find this more efficient than clicking on the tools.

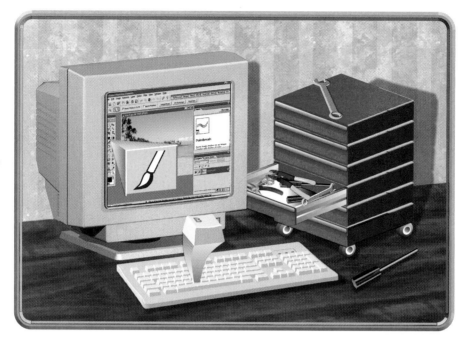

Each tool in the toolbox has a letter associated with it. Elements allows you to easily determine this letter.

USING SHORTCUTS TO SELECT TOOLS

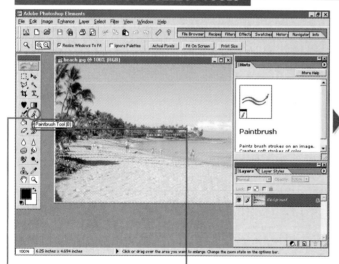

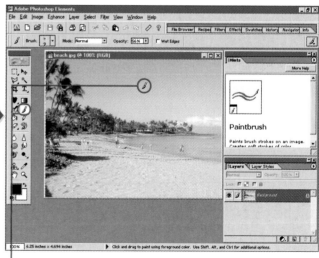

1 Place the cursor (⬚) over a tool in the toolbox and hold it there.

■ A small box appears that describes the tool and gives its shortcut key.

2 Press the indicated letter to select the tool.

■ Elements automatically selects the tool icon in the toolbox and ⬚ switches to the new tool.

Note: You can modify the shape of the cursor by adjusting Photoshop's Preferences settings. See Chapter 1 for more information.

■ You can use the following shortcut keys to activate common Photoshop tools:

M Marquee	**V** Move
L Lasso	**B** Paintbrush
T Type	**Z** Zoom

You can click buttons on the Shortcuts bar to avoid having to go to the menus to execute commands.

USING THE SHORTCUTS BAR

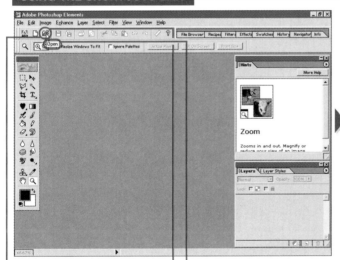

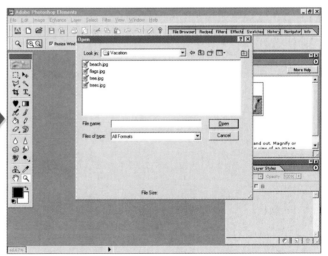

1 Place ⬚ over a button in the Shortcuts bar and hold it there.

■ A small box appears that describes the shortcut.

2 Click the button.

■ Elements executes the command.

■ The following are some of the commands accessible on the Shortcuts bar:

🗁 Open   💾 Save

🖨 Print   ✄ Cut

📋 Paste   ❓ Help

UNDO COMMANDS

You can undo multiple commands by using the History palette, which allows you to correct mistakes.

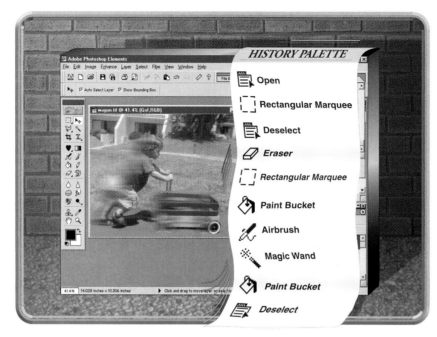

HISTORY PALETTE

- Open
- Rectangular Marquee
- Deselect
- Eraser
- Rectangular Marquee
- Paint Bucket
- Airbrush
- Magic Wand
- Paint Bucket
- Deselect

The History palette lists recently executed commands with the most recent command at the bottom.

UNDO COMMANDS

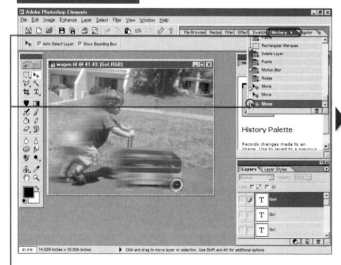

1 Click the **History** tab.

2 Click and drag the History slider (▷) upward.

■ Alternatively, you can click a previous command in the History palette.

■ Photoshop undoes the previous commands.

REVERT AN IMAGE

You can revert an
image to the
previously saved
state. This allows
you to start your
image editing over.

REVERT AN IMAGE

1 Click **File**.

2 Click **Revert**.

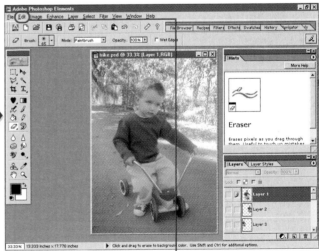

■ Photoshop reverts the
image to its previously
saved state.

■ You can click **Edit** and
then **Undo Revert** to return
to the unreverted state.

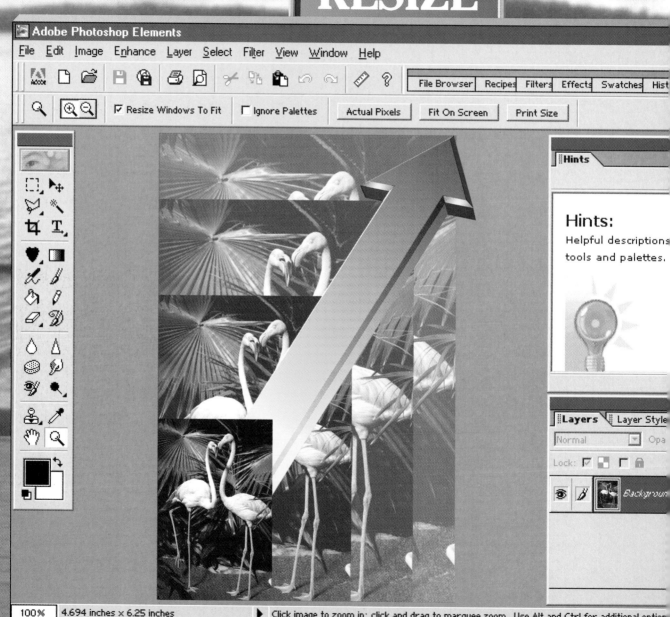

CHAPTER 3

Changing the Size of an Image

Would you like to change the size of your image? This chapter shows you how to change the on-screen size or print size, how to change the print resolution, and how to crop an image.

CHANGE THE ON-SCREEN SIZE OF AN IMAGE

You can change the size at which an image displays on computer monitors so that viewers can see the entire image.

Because you lose less detail when you decrease an image's size than when you increase it, consider starting your editing with an image that is too big rather than one that is too small.

CHANGE THE ON-SCREEN SIZE OF AN IMAGE

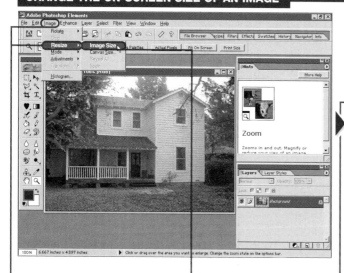

1 Click **Image**.

2 Click **Resize**.

3 Click **Image Size**.

■ The Image Size dialog box appears listing the height and width of the image in pixels.

■ To resize by a certain percentage, click ▾ (♦) and change the units to **percent**.

4 Make sure that you click **Resample Image** (☐ changes to ☑).

Note: Resampling *is the process of increasing or decreasing the number of pixels in an image.*

46

What is the difference between an image's on-screen size and its print size?

On-screen size depends only on the number of pixels that make up an image. Print size depends on the number of pixels as well as the print resolution, which is the density of the pixels on a printed page. Given the same on-screen size, higher resolutions print a smaller image, while lower resolutions print a larger image.

96 ppi - Windows   72 ppi - Mac

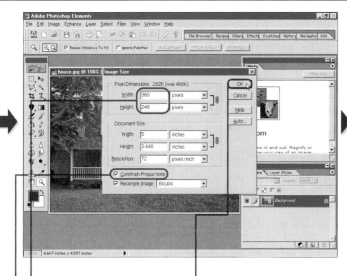

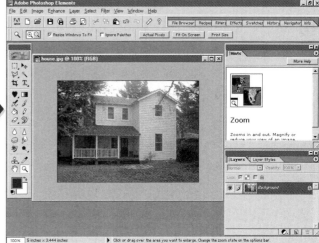

5 Type a size for a dimension.

■ You can click **Constrain Proportions** (☐ changes to ☑) to cause the other dimension to change proportionally.

6 Click **OK**.

■ You can restore the original dialog box settings by pressing and holding down Alt (option) and clicking **Cancel**, which changes to **Reset**.

■ Elements resizes the image.

Note: Changing the number of pixels in an image can add blur. To sharpen a resized image, apply the Unsharp Mask filter as covered in Chapter 10.

CHANGE THE PRINT SIZE OF AN IMAGE

You can change the printed size of an image to determine how it appears on paper.

CHANGE THE PRINT SIZE OF AN IMAGE

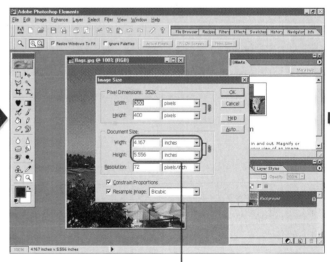

1 Click **Image**.

2 Click **Resize**.

3 Click **Image Size**.

■ The Image Size dialog box appears listing the current height and width of the printed image.

■ You can click ▼ (⬥) to change the unit of measurement.

How do I preview an image's printed size?

Click **File** and then click **Print Preview.** A dialog box displays how the image will print on the page. There are also commands that let you adjust the size and positioning of the image.

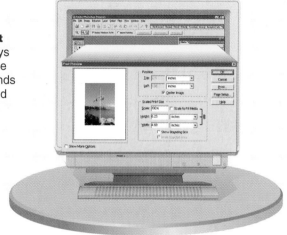

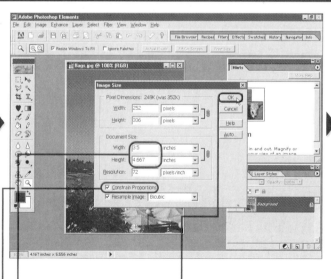

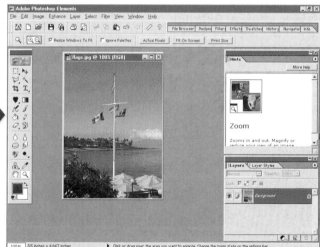

4 Type a size for a dimension.

■ You can click **Constrain Proportions** (☐ changes to ☑) to cause the other dimension to change proportionally.

5 Click **OK**.

■ You can restore the original dialog box settings by pressing and holding down Alt (option) and clicking **Cancel**, which changes to **Reset**.

■ Elements resizes the image.

Note: Changing the number of pixels in an image can add blur. To sharpen a resized image, apply the Unsharp Mask filter as covered in Chapter 10.

CHANGE THE RESOLUTION OF AN IMAGE

You can change the print resolution of an image to increase or decrease the print quality.

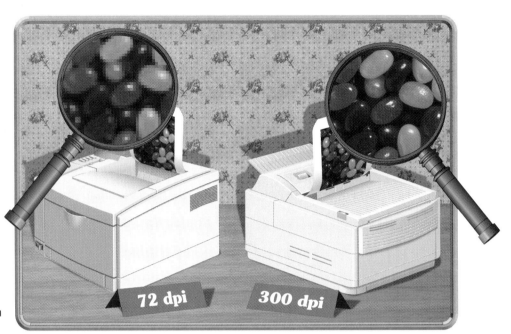

72 dpi   300 dpi

The resolution, combined with the number of pixels in an image, determines the size of a printed image.

The greater the resolution, the better the image looks on the printed page — up to a limit, which varies with the type of printer.

CHANGE THE RESOLUTION OF AN IMAGE

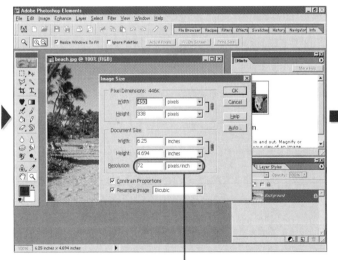

1 Click **Image**.

2 Click **Resize**.

3 Click **Image Size**.

■ The Image Size dialog box appears listing the current resolution of the image.

■ You can click ▼ (♦) to change the resolution units.

What is the relationship between resolution, on-screen size, and print size?

To determine the printed size of a Photoshop image, you can divide the on-screen size by the resolution. If you have an image with an on-screen width of 480 pixels and a resolution of 120 pixels per inch, the printed width is 4 inches.

480 pixels/120 pixels per inch =4 inches

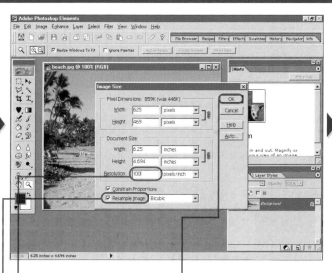

4 Type a new resolution.

■ You can click **Resample Image** (☐ changes to ☑) to adjust the number of pixels in your image and keep the printed dimensions fixed.

5 Click **OK**.

■ You can restore the original dialog box settings by pressing and holding down Alt (option) and clicking **Cancel**, which changes to **Reset**.

■ In this example, because the change in resolution changes the number of pixels in the image, the on-screen image changes in size while the print size stays the same.

CHANGE THE CANVAS SIZE OF AN IMAGE

You can alter the canvas size of an image in order to change its rectangular shape or add blank space around its borders.

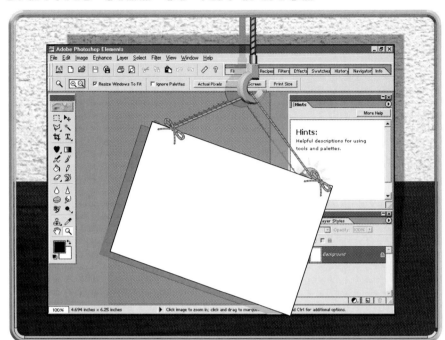

The *canvas* is the area on which an image sits. Changing the canvas size is one way to crop an image.

The Crop tool gives you an alternative to changing the canvas size. See the section "Crop an Image" for more information.

CHANGE THE CANVAS SIZE OF AN IMAGE

1 Click **Image**.

2 Click **Resize**.

3 Click **Canvas Size**.

■ The Canvas Size dialog box displays, listing the current dimensions of the canvas.

■ You can click ▾ (◆) to change the unit of measurement.

Why would I want to change the canvas size instead of using the crop tool?

You may find changing the canvas size useful when you want to change the size of an image precisely. You can specify the exact number of pixels that Elements adds or subtracts around the border. With the Crop tool, you may find it more difficult to make changes with pixel precision.

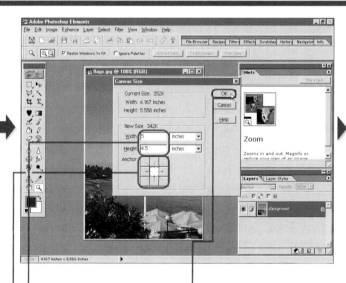

4 Type the new canvas dimensions.

■ You can modify in which directions Elements changes the canvas size by selecting an anchor point.

5 Click **OK**.

*Note: If you decrease a dimension, Elements displays a dialog box asking whether you want to proceed. Click **Proceed**.*

■ Elements changes the image's canvas size.

■ Because the middle anchor point was selected in this example, the canvas size changes equally on all sides.

■ Elements fills any new canvas space with the background color — in this case, white.

CROP AN IMAGE

You can use the Crop tool to change the size of an image and remove unneeded space on the sides.

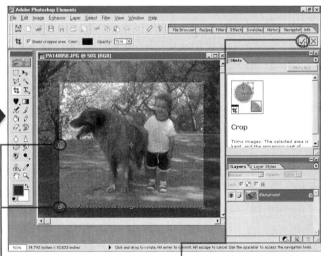

1 Click the Crop tool ( ).

2 Click and drag your cursor ( ) to select the area of the image you want to keep.

■ You can also crop an image by changing its canvas size.

Note: See the section "Change the Canvas Size of an Image" for more information.

3 Click and drag the side and corner handles ( ) to adjust the size of the cropping boundary.

■ You can click and drag inside the cropping boundary to move it without adjusting its size.

4 Click or press **Enter** (**Return**).

■ To exit the cropping process, you can press **Esc** (⌘ + .).

How do I increase the area of an image using the Crop tool?

Enlarge the image window to add extra window space around the image. Then apply the Crop tool so that the cropping boundary extends beyond the borders of the image. When you apply cropping, the image canvas enlarges.

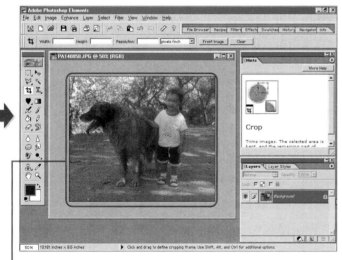

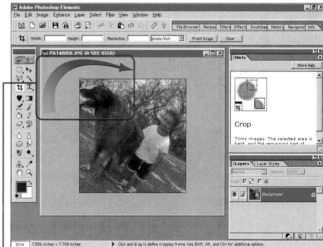

■ Elements crops the image, deleting the pixels outside of the cropping boundary.

ROTATE THE CROPPING AREA

1 Perform Steps 1 through 3 on the previous pages.

2 Click and drag outside of the boundary lines.

3 Click ✓ or press `Enter` (`Return`).

■ Elements rotates the cropping boundary before cropping the image.

CHAPTER 4

Making Selections

Do you want to move, color, or transform parts of your image independently from the rest of the image? The first step is to make a selection. This chapter shows you how.

SELECT WITH THE MARQUEE TOOLS

You can select a rectangular or elliptical area of your image by using the Marquee tools. Then you can move, delete, or stylize the selected area using other Photoshop commands.

SELECT WITH THE MARQUEE TOOLS

USING THE RECTANGULAR MARQUEE TOOL

1 Click the Rectangular Marquee tool ([⬚]).

2 Click and drag your cursor (+) diagonally inside the image window.

■ You can hold down **Shift** while you click and drag to create a square selection.

■ Elements selects a rectangular portion of your image.

■ You can now perform other commands on the selection.

■ You can deselect a selection by clicking **Select** and then **Deselect**.

58

How do I customize the Marquee tools?

You can customize the Marquee tools (⬚ and ◯) by using the boxes and menus in the Options bar. Typing in a Feather value softens your selection edge — which means that Elements partially selects pixels near the edge. The Style list lets you define your Marquee tool as a fixed size. You define the fixed dimensions in the Width and Height boxes.

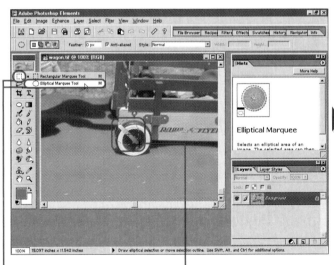

USING THE ELLIPTICAL MARQUEE TOOL

1 Click and hold the (⬚).

2 From the box that appears, click the Elliptical Marquee tool (◯).

3 Click and drag + diagonally inside the image window.

■ You can press and hold down **Shift** while you click and drag to create a circular selection.

■ Elements selects an elliptical portion of your image.

■ You can now perform other commands on the selection.

■ You can deselect a selection by clicking **Select** and then **Deselect**.

SELECT WITH THE LASSO TOOL

You can create oddly shaped selections with the Lasso tools. Then you can move, delete, or stylize the selected area using other Photoshop commands.

You can use the regular Lasso tool to create curved selections. The Polygonal Lasso tool lets you easily create a selection made up of many straight lines.

SELECT WITH THE LASSO TOOL

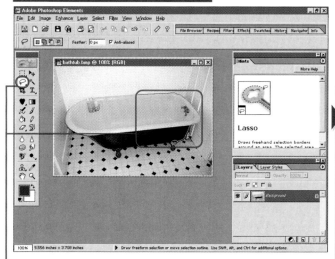

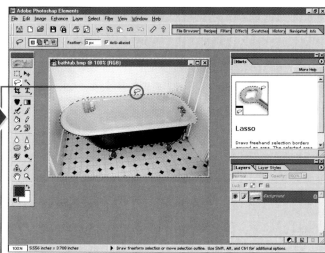

USING THE REGULAR LASSO

1 Click the Lasso tool (⌀).

2 Click and drag with your cursor (⌀) to make a selection.

■ To accurately trace a complicated edge, you can magnify that part of the image with the Zoom tool (🔍).

Note: See Chapter 2 for more on the Zoom tool.

3 Drag to the beginning point and release the mouse button.

■ The selection is now complete.

What if my lasso selection is not as precise as I want it to be?

You may find selecting complicated outlines with the Lasso tool ( ) difficult, even with the steadiest of hands. To fix an imprecise Lasso selection, you can

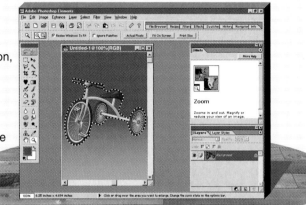

- Deselect the selection by clicking **Select** and then **Deselect** and try again.

- Try to fix your selection. See the section "Add to or Subtract from Your Selection" for more information.

- Switch to the Magnetic Lasso. See the section "Select with the Magnetic Lasso Tool" for more on the use of this tool.

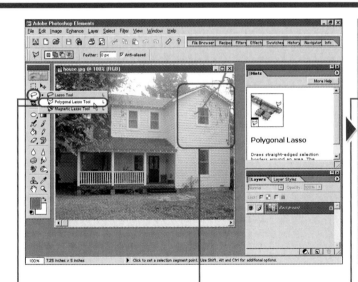

USING THE POLYGONAL LASSO

1 Click and hold .

2 Click the Polygonal Lasso tool ( ) in the box that appears.

3 Click multiple times along the border of the area you want to select.

4 To complete the selection, click the starting point.

■ You can also double-click anywhere in the image and Elements adds a final straight line connected to the starting point.

■ The selection is now complete.

■ You can achieve a polygonal effect with the regular Lasso tool by pressing Alt (option) and clicking to make your selection.

SELECT WITH THE MAGNETIC LASSO TOOL

You can select elements of your image that have well-defined edges quickly and easily with the Magnetic Lasso tool.

The Magnetic Lasso works best when the element you are trying to select contrasts sharply with its background.

SELECT WITH THE MAGNETIC LASSO TOOL

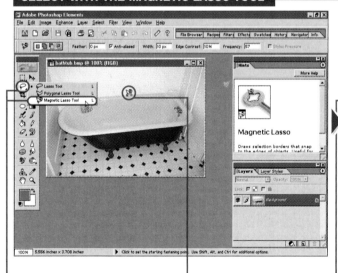

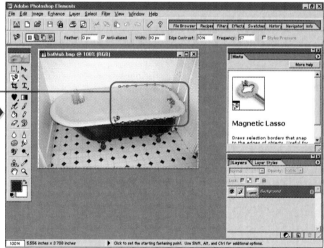

1 Click and hold the 🔲.

2 Click the Magnetic Lasso tool (🔲) from the box that appears.

3 Click the edge of the object you want to select.

■ This creates a beginning anchor point.

4 Drag your cursor (🔲) along the edge of the object.

■ The Magnetic Lasso's path snaps to the edge of the object as you drag.

■ To help guide the lasso, you can click to add anchor points as you go along the path.

How can I adjust the precision of the Magnetic Lasso tool?

You can use the Options bar to adjust the Magnetic Lasso tool's precision:

- **Width:** The number of nearby pixels the lasso considers when creating a selection.

- **Edge Contrast:** How much contrast is required for the lasso to consider something an edge.

- **Frequency:** The frequency of the anchor points.

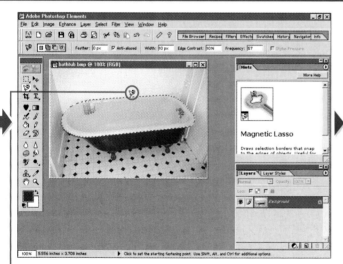

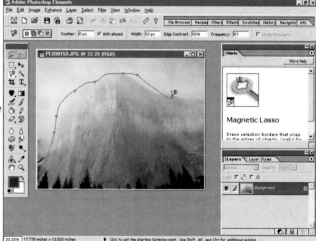

5 Click the beginning anchor point to finish your selection.

■ Alternatively, you can double-click anywhere in the image and Elements completes the selection for you.

■ The path is complete.

■ This example shows that the Magnetic Lasso is less useful for selecting areas where you find little contrast between the image and its background.

SELECT WITH THE MAGIC WAND TOOL

You can select groups of similarly colored pixels with the Magic Wand tool. You may find this useful if you want to remove an object from a background.

You can control how similar a pixel is and whether Elements selects it by selecting an appropriate tolerance value.

SELECT WITH THE MAGIC WAND TOOL

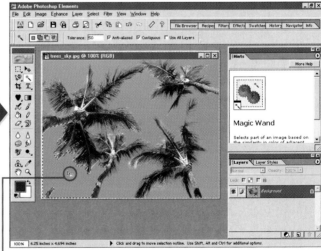

1 Click the Magic Wand tool (🔍).

2 Type a number from 0 to 255 into the Tolerance field.

■ To select a narrow range of colors, type a small number; to select a wide range of colors, type a large number.

3 Click the area you want to select inside the image.

■ Elements selects the pixel you clicked, plus any similarly colored pixels near it.

With what type of images does the Magic Wand work best?

The Magic Wand tool (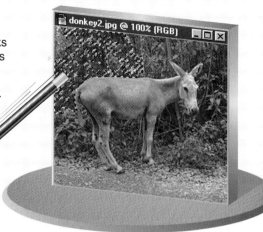) works best with images that have areas of solid color. The Magic Wand tool is less helpful with images that contain subtle shifts in color or color gradients.

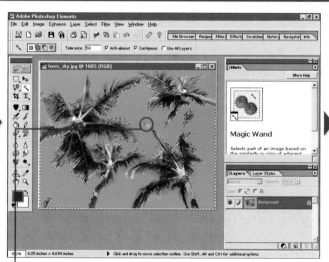

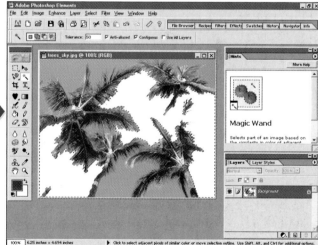

■ 4 To add to your selection, press **Shift** and click elsewhere in the image.

■ Photoshop adds to your selection.

■ 5 To delete the selected pixels, press **Delete**.

■ Elements replaces the pixels with the background color.

■ In this example, Elements replaces the pixels with white.

■ If you make the selection in a layer, the deleted selection becomes transparent.

SELECT ALL THE PIXELS IN AN IMAGE

You can select all
the pixels in an
image by using a
single command.
This lets you
perform a command
on the entire image,
such as copying it to
a different image
window.

With the entire
image window
selected, you
can easily delete
your image or copy
and paste it into
another window.

SELECT ALL THE PIXELS IN AN IMAGE

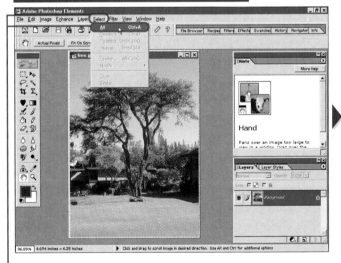

■1 Click **Select**.

■2 Click **All**.

■ You can also press Ctrl +
A (⌘ + A) to select all the
pixels in an image.

■ Elements selects the
entire image window.

■ You can delete your
image by pressing Delete.

■ To copy your image, press
Ctrl + C (⌘ + C).

■ To paste your image,
press Ctrl + V (⌘ + V).

MOVE A SELECTION BORDER

You can move a selection
border if your original
selection is not in the
intended place.

MOVE A SELECTION BORDER

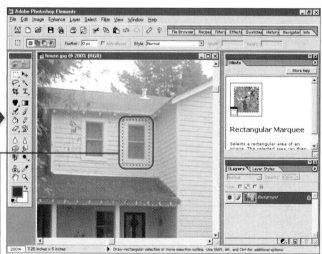

1 Make a selection
with a selection tool
(, , or).

*Note: To learn more about the
various selection tools, see the
previous sections in this chapter.*

2 Click and drag inside the
selection.

■ The selection border
moves.

■ You can hide a selection
by clicking **View** and then
Selection Edges.

ADD TO OR SUBTRACT FROM YOUR SELECTION

You can add to or subtract from your selection by using various selection tools.

ADD TO A SELECTION

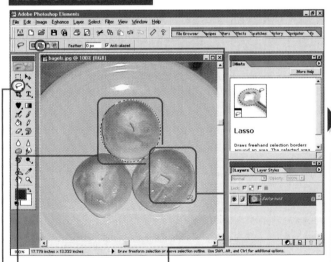

1 Make a selection using one of Elements' selection tools.

■ The selection in this example illustrates the use of the Lasso tool.

2 Click a selection tool.

Note: See the previous sections in this chapter to select the appropriate tool for your image.

3 Click the Add to Selection button (▣).

4 Select the area you want to add.

5 Complete the selection by closing the path.

■ The original selection enlarges.

■ You can enlarge the selection further by repeating Steps **2** through **5**.

■ You can also add to a selection by pressing **Shift** as you make your selection.

What tools can I use to add to or subtract from a selection?

You can use any of the Marquee, Lasso, or Magic Wand tools, discussed in previous sections in this chapter, to add to or subtract from a selection. All three have Add to Selection and Subtract from Selection buttons available in the Options bar when you activate them.

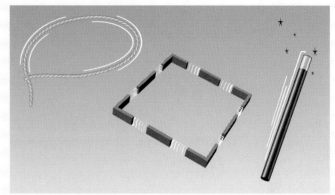

SUBTRACT FROM A SELECTION

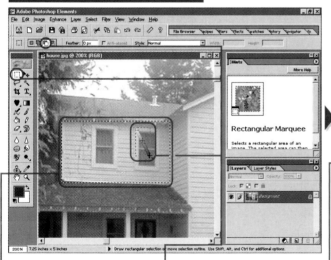
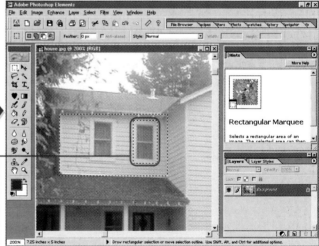

1 Make a selection using one of Elements' selection tools.

■ The selection in this example illustrates the use of the Rectangular Marquee tool.

2 Click a selection tool.

3 Click the Subtract from Selection button (▣).

4 Select the area you want to subtract.

■ Elements deselects, or subtracts, the selected area.

■ You can subtract other parts of the selection by repeating Steps **2** through **4**.

■ You can also subtract from a selection by pressing and holding down Alt (option) as you make your selection.

EXPAND OR CONTRACT SELECTIONS

You can expand or contract a selection by a set number of pixels. This lets you easily fine-tune your selections.

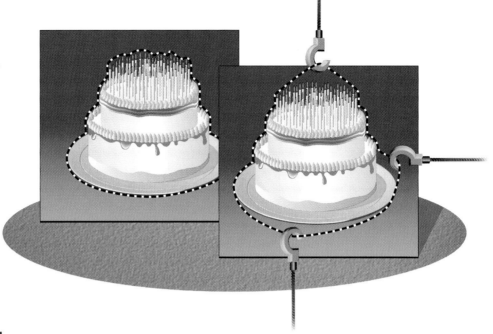

You can expand or contract a selection up to 100 pixels at a time.

EXPAND A SELECTION

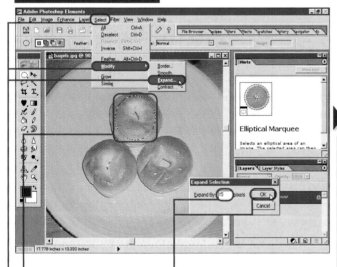

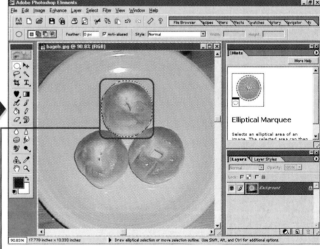

1 Make a selection using one of Elements' selection tools.

2 Click **Select**.

3 Click **Modify**.

4 Click **Expand**.

■ The Expand Selection dialog box appears.

5 Type a value in the Expand By field.

6 Click **OK**.

■ Elements expands the selection by the specified number of pixels.

■ You can repeat Steps **2** through **6** to expand a selection further.

How can I smooth the edges of a selection?

Make your selection and then click **Select, Modify,** and **Smooth.** Type a Sample Radius value. The greater the value, the more Elements smoothes the selection.

CONTRACT A SELECTION

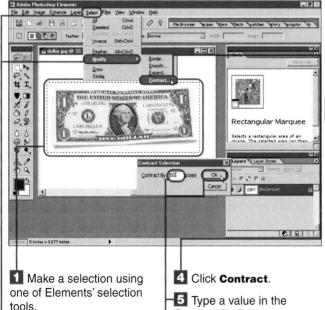

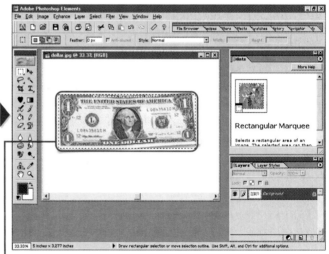

1 Make a selection using one of Elements' selection tools.

2 Click **Select**.

3 Click **Modify**.

4 Click **Contract**.

5 Type a value in the Contract By field.

6 Click **OK**.

■ Elements contracts the selection by the number of pixels specified.

■ You can repeat Steps **2** through **6** to contract a selection further.

INVERT A SELECTION

You can invert a selection to deselect what is currently selected and select everything else. This is useful when you want to select a background around an object.

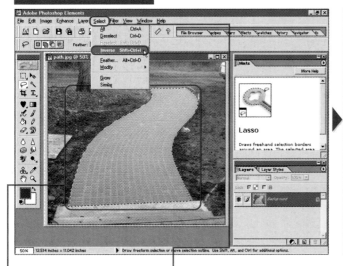

1 Make a selection using one of Elements' selection tools.

2 Click **Select**.

3 Click **Inverse**.

■ Elements inverts the selection.

GROW A SELECTION

You can increase
the size of your
selection using the
Grow command,
which is useful when
you want to include
similarly colored,
neighboring pixels
in your selection.

GROW A SELECTION

1 Make a selection using
one of Elements' selection
tools.

2 Click **Select**.

3 Click **Grow**.

■ The selection expands to
include similarly colored
pixels contiguous with the
current selection.

■ To include noncontiguous
pixels as well, you can click
Select and then **Similar**.

APPLYING DISTORT

DELETING SELECTION

PASTING SELECTION IN NEW WINDOW

...NOW APPLYING TRANSFORMATION...

CLOSE

MOVE SELECTION

CHAPTER 5

Manipulating Selections

Making a selection defines a specific area of your Photoshop image. This chapter shows you how to move, stretch, erase, and manipulate your selection in a variety of ways.

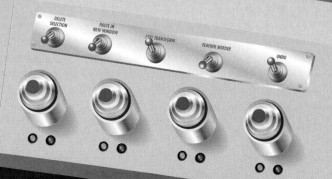

MOVE A SELECTION

You can move
a selection by
using the Move
tool, which lets
you rearrange
elements of
your image.

You can place
elements of your
image either
in their own
background or
in layers. For
details about
layers, see
Chapter 8.

MOVE A SELECTION

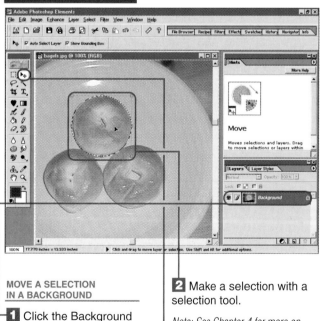

**MOVE A SELECTION
IN A BACKGROUND**

1 Click the Background
layer in the Layers palette.

■ If you start with a
newly scanned image,
the Background layer is
probably your only layer.

2 Make a selection with a
selection tool.

*Note: See Chapter 4 for more on
using selection tools and Chapter 8
for more on layers.*

3 Click the Move tool ( ).

4 Click inside the selection
and drag.

■ Elements fills the former
location of the selection with
the current background
color.

■ In this example, white is
the background color.

How do I move a selection in a straight line?

Hold down the Shift key while you drag with the Move tool (). Doing so constrains the movement of your selection horizontally, vertically, or diagonally — depending on the direction you drag.

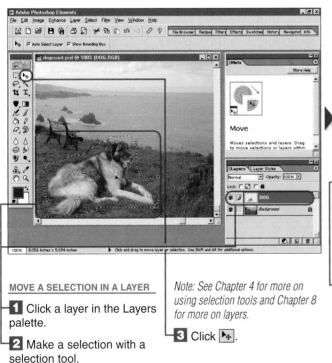

MOVE A SELECTION IN A LAYER

1 Click a layer in the Layers palette.

2 Make a selection with a selection tool.

Note: See Chapter 4 for more on using selection tools and Chapter 8 for more on layers.

3 Click ⊕.

4 Click inside the selection and drag.

■ Elements moves the image.

■ Elements fills the original location of the selection with transparent pixels.

■ Unlike the background — Elements' opaque default layer — layers can include transparent pixels.

COPY AND PASTE A SELECTION

You can copy a selection
and make a duplicate
of it somewhere else in
the image.

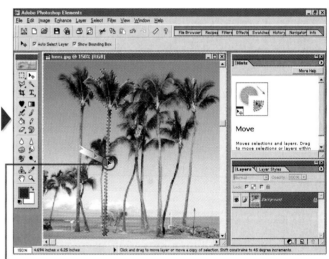

**USING THE KEYBOARD
AND MOUSE**

1 Make a selection with a
selection tool.

*Note: See Chapter 4 for more on
using selection tools.*

2 Click ⌖.

3 Press Alt (option) while
you click and drag the
selection.

4 Release the mouse
button to "drop" the
selection.

■ Elements creates a
duplicate of the selection
and moves it to the new
location.

How can I copy a selection from one window to another?

Click , press **Alt** (**option**), and click and drag your selection from one window to another. You can also copy selections between windows by using the **Copy** and **Paste** commands in the **Edit** menu.

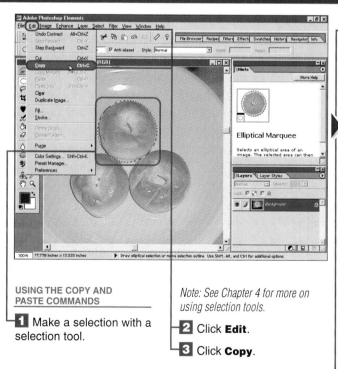

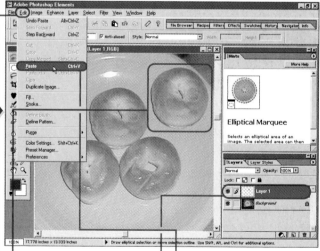

USING THE COPY AND PASTE COMMANDS

1 Make a selection with a selection tool.

Note: See Chapter 4 for more on using selection tools.

2 Click **Edit**.

3 Click **Copy**.

4 Using a selection tool, select where you want to paste the copied element.

■ If you do not select an area, Elements pastes the copy over the original.

5 Click **Edit**.

6 Click **Paste**.

■ Elements pastes the copy into a new layer, which you can now move independently of the original image.

Note: See the section "Move a Selection" for more on moving your image.

DELETE A SELECTION

You can delete a
selection to remove
elements from your
image.

DELETE A SELECTION

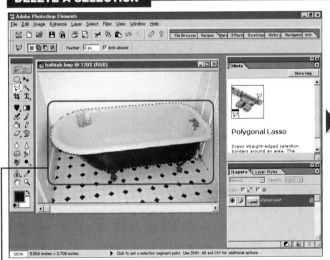

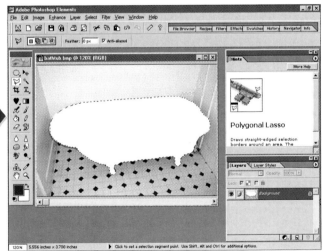

■1■ Make a selection with a
selection tool.

*Note: See Chapter 4 for more on
using selection tools.*

■2■ Press Delete.

■ Elements deletes the
selection.

■ If you are working in
the background layer, the
empty selection fills with the
background color — in this
example, white, the default
background color.

■ If you are working in
a nonbackground layer,
deleting a selection turns the
selected pixels transparent.

ROTATE A SELECTION

You can rotate a selection to tilt or turn an element upside down in your image.

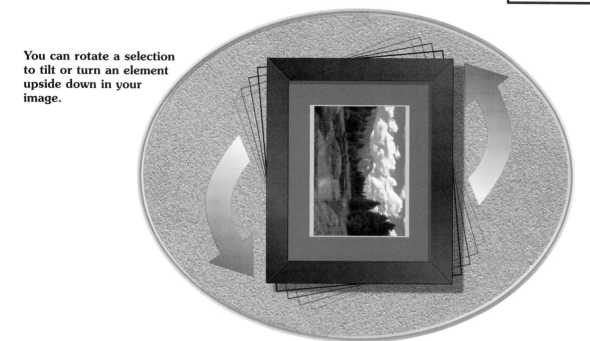

ROTATE A SELECTION

1 Make a selection with a selection tool.

Note: See Chapter 4 for more on using selection tools.

2 Click **Image**.

3 Click **Transform**.

4 Click **Free Transform**.

5 Click and drag to the side of the selection.

■ The selection rotates.

6 Click ✓ or press `Enter` (`Return`) to commit the rotation.

■ You can click ✕ or press `Esc` (⌘ + .) to cancel.

SCALE A SELECTION

You can scale a selection
to make it larger or
smaller. Scaling allows
you to adjust or
emphasize parts
of your image.

1 Make a selection with a
selection tool.

*Note: See Chapter 4 for more on
using selection tools.*

2 Click **Image**.

3 Click **Resize**.

4 Click **Scale**.

■ A rectangular box with
handles on the sides and
corners surrounds the
selection.

5 Click and drag a corner
handle to scale both the
horizontal and vertical axes.

How do I scale both dimensions proportionally?

Hold down Shift while you scale your selection. The two axes of your selection grow or shrink proportionally. This way, Elements does not distort your image.

6 Click and drag a side handle to scale one axis at a time.

7 To apply the scaling, click ✓ or press Enter (Return).

■ To cancel, you can click X or press Esc (⌘ + .).

■ Elements scales the selection to the new dimensions.

SKEW OR DISTORT A SELECTION

You can transform a selection using the Skew or Distort command. This lets you stretch elements in your image into interesting shapes.

SKEW A SELECTION

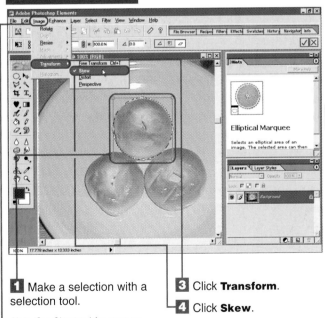

1 Make a selection with a selection tool.

Note: See Chapter 4 for more on using selection tools.

2 Click **Image**.

3 Click **Transform**.

4 Click **Skew**.

■ A rectangular bounding box with handles on the sides and corners surrounds the selection.

5 Click and drag a handle to skew the selection.

■ Because the Skew command works along a single axis, you can drag either horizontally or vertically.

6 To apply the skewing, click ✓ or press **Enter** (**Return**).

■ To cancel, you can click ✗ or press **Esc** (⌘ + .).

How can I undo my skewing or distortion?

You can click **Edit** and then **Undo** to undo the last handle adjustment you made. This is an alternative to clicking ⊠, which cancels the entire Skew or Distort command.

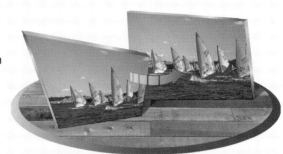

DISTORT A SELECTION

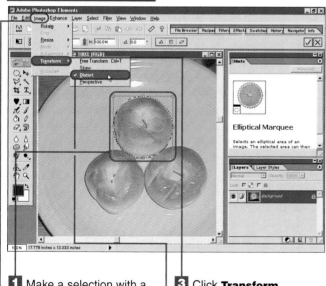

1 Make a selection with a selection tool.

Note: See Chapter 4 for more on using selection tools.

2 Click **Image**.

3 Click **Transform**.

4 Click **Distort**.

■ A rectangular bounding box with handles on the sides and corners surrounds the selection.

5 Click and drag a handle to distort the selection.

■ The Distort command works independently of the selection's different axes; you can drag a handle both vertically and horizontally.

6 To apply the distortion, click ✓ or press **Enter** (**Return**).

■ To cancel, you can click ⊠ or press **Esc** (⌘ + ▪).

USING THE FREE TRANSFORM TOOL

You can use the Free Transform tool to scale and rotate a selection all at once.

To apply the scale or rotate commands independently, see the section "Scale a Selection" or "Rotate a Selection."

USING THE FREE TRANSFORM TOOL

1 Make a selection with a selection tool.

Note: See Chapter 4 for more on using selection tools.

2 Click **Image**.

3 Click **Transform**.

4 Click **Free Transform**.

■ A rectangular bounding box with handles on the sides and corners surrounds the selection.

5 Click and drag a corner handle to scale the selection in two dimensions.

■ You can also click and drag a side handle to scale it in one dimension.

How can I easily switch between the different transformation tools?

You can click the transformation buttons located in the Options bar. This lets you switch between the Rotate (⊿), Scale (▣), and Skew (◿) tools.

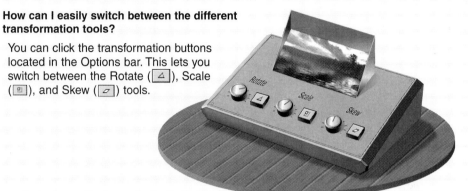

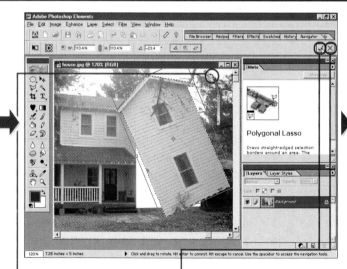

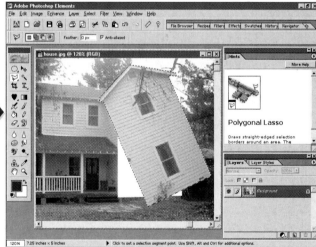

6 Click and drag outside the selection to rotate it.

7 To apply the distortion, click ✓ or press **Enter** (**Return**).

■ To cancel, you can click ✕ or press **Esc** (⌘ + .).

■ Elements applies your changes.

FEATHER THE BORDER OF A SELECTION

You can feather a selection's border to create soft edges.

To soften edges, you must first select an object, feather the selection border, and then delete the part of the image that surrounds your selection.

FEATHER THE BORDER OF A SELECTION

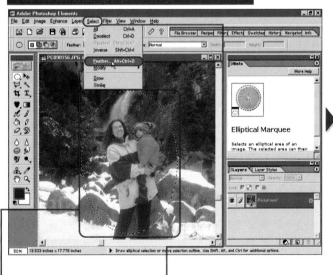

SELECT AND FEATHER THE IMAGE

1 Make a selection with a selection tool.

Note: See Chapter 4 for more on using selection tools.

2 Click **Select**.

3 Click **Feather**.

■ The Feather Selection dialog box appears.

4 Type a pixel value to determine the softness of the edge.

5 Click **OK**.

What happens if I feather a selection and then apply a command to it?

Elements applies the command only partially to pixels near the edge of the selection.

DELETE THE SURROUNDING BACKGROUND

6 Click **Select**.

7 Click **Inverse**.

■ The selection inverts, but still feathers.

8 Press Delete.

■ You can now see the effect of the feathering.

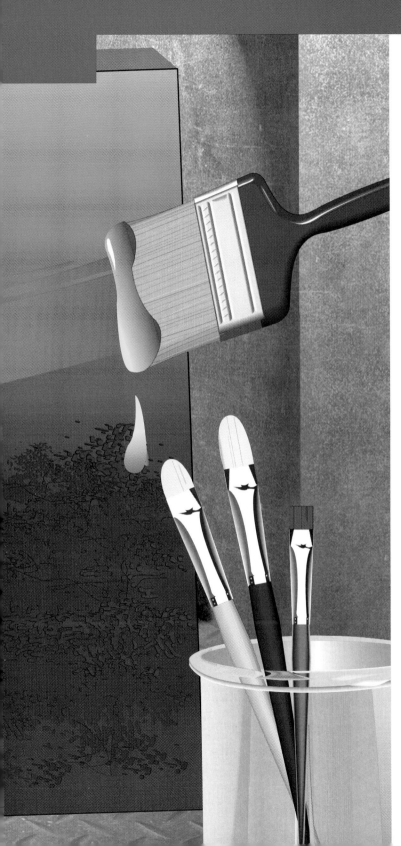

CHAPTER 6

Painting and Drawing with Color

Want to add splashes, streaks, or solid areas of color to your image? Elements offers a variety of tools with which you can add almost any color imaginable. This chapter introduces you to those tools and shows you how to choose your colors.

You can select two colors to work with at a time in Elements — a foreground color and a background color. Painting tools such as the Paintbrush apply foreground color. You apply the background color when you use the Eraser tool, enlarge the image canvas, or cut pieces out of your image.

SELECT THE FOREGROUND COLOR

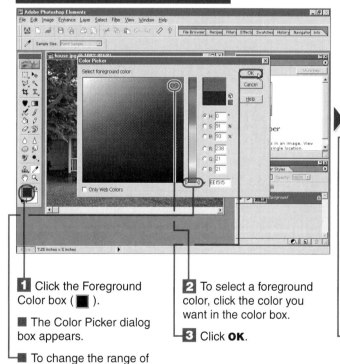

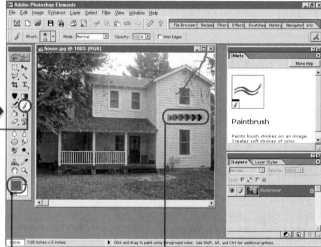

1 Click the Foreground Color box (■).

■ The Color Picker dialog box appears.

■ To change the range of colors that appears in the color box, click and drag the slider (▷).

2 To select a foreground color, click the color you want in the color box.

3 Click **OK**.

■ The selected color appears in the Foreground Color box.

4 Click a painting tool in the toolbox.

■ This example uses the Paintbrush tool (✏).

Note: To learn more about painting tools, see the section "Using the Paintbrush Tool."

5 Click and drag your cursor (○) to apply the color.

How do I reset the foreground and background colors?

Click the Default icon () to the lower left of the Foreground and Background icons. Doing so resets the colors to black and white.

SELECT THE BACKGROUND COLOR

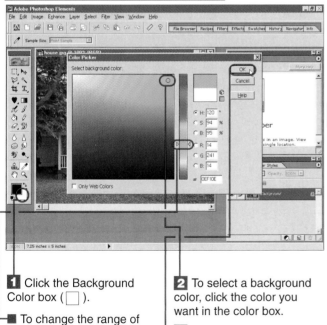

1 Click the Background Color box (☐).

■ To change the range of colors that appears in the box, click and drag ▷.

2 To select a background color, click the color you want in the color box.

3 Click **OK**.

4 Click the Eraser tool (⬚).

5 Click and drag your cursor (⬚).

■ The tool "erases" by painting with the background color.

Note: In non-background layers, the eraser turns pixels transparent. See Chapter 8 for a full discussion of layers.

SELECT A WEB-SAFE COLOR

You can select one of the 216 Web-safe colors as a foreground or background color. A Web-safe color displays accurately in all Web browsers, no matter what type of monitor or operating system a user has.

See Chapter 13 for information about saving images with Web-safe colors.

SELECT A WEB-SAFE COLOR

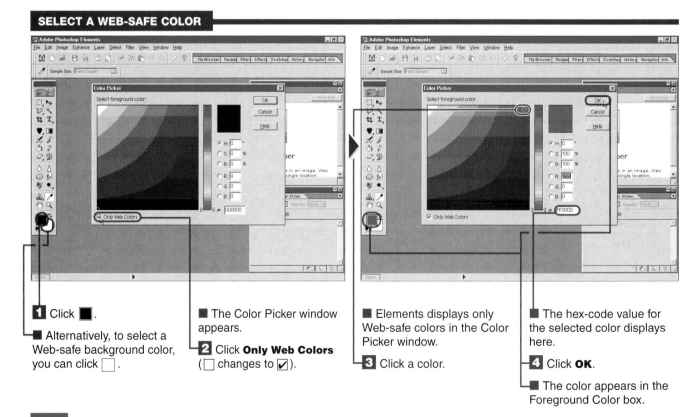

1 Click ■.

■ Alternatively, to select a Web-safe background color, you can click ☐.

■ The Color Picker window appears.

2 Click **Only Web Colors** (☐ changes to ☑).

■ Elements displays only Web-safe colors in the Color Picker window.

3 Click a color.

■ The hex-code value for the selected color displays here.

4 Click **OK**.

■ The color appears in the Foreground Color box.

SELECT A COLOR WITH THE EYEDROPPER TOOL

You can select a color
from an open image with
the Eyedropper tool. The
Eyedropper tool enables
you to paint using a
color already present in
your image.

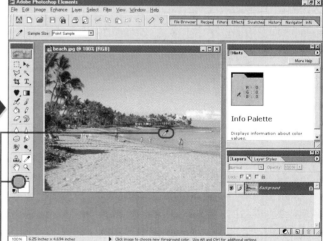

SELECT A COLOR WITH THE EYEDROPPER TOOL

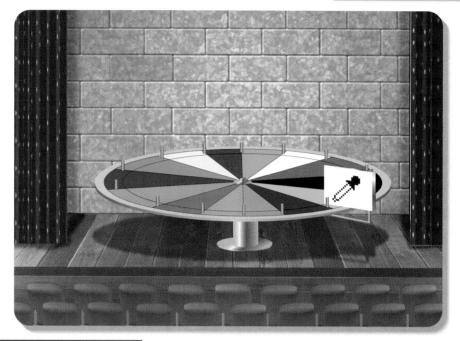

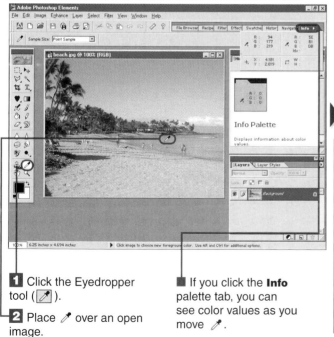

1 Click the Eyedropper
tool ( ).

2 Place   over an open
image.

■ If you click the **Info**
palette tab, you can
see color values as you
move .

3 Click to select the
color of the pixel beneath
the   tip.

■ The color becomes the
new foreground color.

■ To select a new
background color, you
can press **Alt** (**option**)
as you click the color in
step **3**.

SELECT A COLOR WITH THE SWATCHES PALETTE

You can select a color with the Swatches palette. The Swatches palette lets you choose from a small set of commonly used colors.

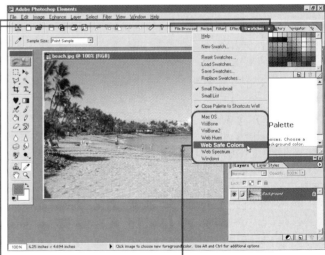

SELECT A COLOR WITH THE SWATCHES PALETTE

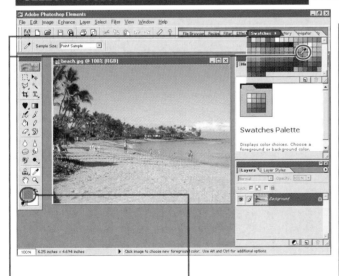

SELECT A COLOR

1 Click the **Swatches** palette tab.

2 Click a color swatch to select a foreground color.

■ The color becomes the new foreground color.

■ To select a background color, press Alt (option) as you click a color swatch in step **2**.

CHANGE THE SWATCH SELECTION

1 Click the **Swatches** palette tab.

2 Click ▶.

3 Click a swatch set.

■ The set of swatches appears in the Swatches palette.

96

STORE A COLOR IN THE SWATCHES PALETTE

You can add custom
colors to the Swatches
palette. This enables you
to easily select these
colors later.

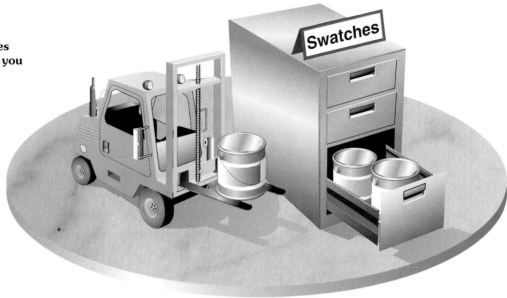

STORE A COLOR IN THE SWATCHES PALETTE

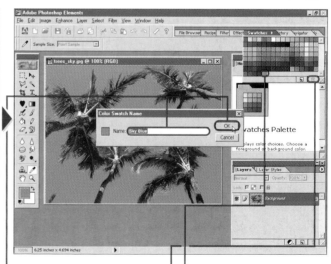

1 Click 🖋.

2 Click inside the image to select a color.

3 Click the **Swatches** palette tab.

4 Place 🖋 over an empty area of the Swatches palette (🖋 changes to 👆).

5 Click to add the color.

■ The Color Swatch Name dialog box appears.

6 Type a name for the new color swatch.

7 Click **OK**.

■ Elements adds the color as a new swatch.

■ You can remove a swatch by clicking it and dragging it to the Trash can (🗑).

USING THE PAINTBRUSH TOOL

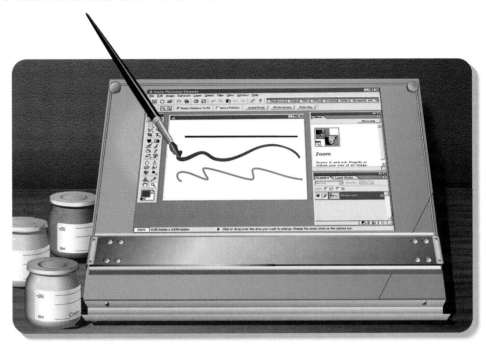

You can use the Paintbrush tool to add color to your image. You may find the paintbrush useful for applying bands of color.

To limit where the paintbrush applies color, create a selection before painting. For details, see Chapter 4.

USING THE PAINTBRUSH TOOL

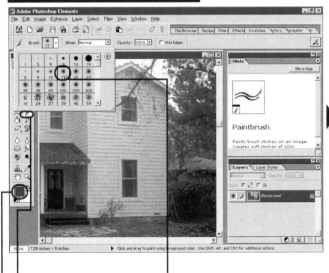

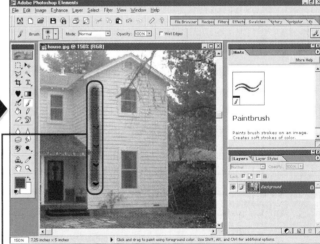

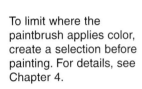

1 Click the Paintbrush tool (✐).

2 Click ■ to select a color with which to paint.

Note: For details, see the section "Select the Foreground and Background Colors."

3 Click the Brush ⊡ and select a brush size and type.

4 Click and drag ○ to apply the foreground color to the image.

■ To undo the most recent brush stroke, you can click **Edit** and then **Undo Paintbrush**.

Note: To undo more than one brush stroke, see Chapter 2 to learn how to use the History palette.

How do I paint thin lines?

You can use the Pencil tool ( ), which is similar to the Paintbrush tool ( ) except that it paints only thin, hard-edged lines. Like the Paintbrush, the Pencil applies the foreground color.

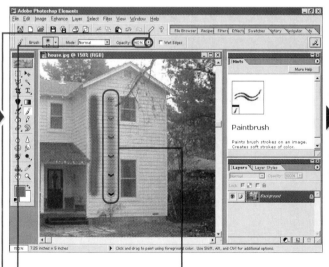

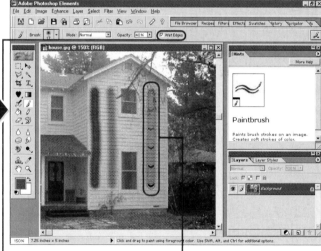

5 Type a percentage value to change the opacity of the brush strokes.

■ Alternatively, you can click the Opacity ▶ and adjust the slider.

6 Click and drag ○ to apply the semitransparent paintbrush.

7 Click **Wet Edges** to concentrate the paint at the edges (☐ changes to ☑).

8 Click and drag ○ to apply the customized paintbrush.

CHANGE BRUSH STYLES

You can select from a variety of predefined brush styles to apply color in different ways. You can also create a custom brush style.

CHANGE BRUSH STYLES

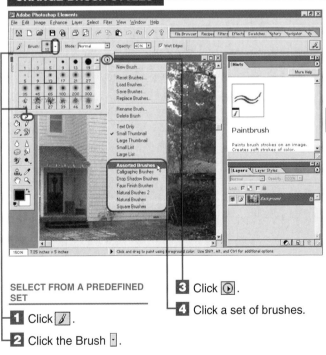

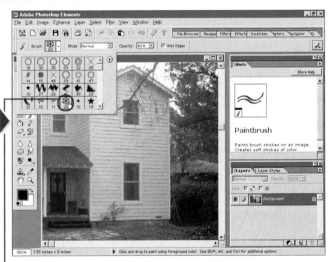

SELECT FROM A PREDEFINED SET

1 Click ![brush].

2 Click the Brush ▾.

3 Click ![arrow].

4 Click a set of brushes.

■ The set appears in the brush menu.

5 Click a brush style to select it.

Note: To apply the brush, see the section "Using the Paintbrush Tool."

How can I make a brush apply dots instead of a line?

Click the brush icon in the Options bar, such as , and increase the Spacing value to greater than 100%. When you click and drag your cursor, you get a discontiguous brush stroke.

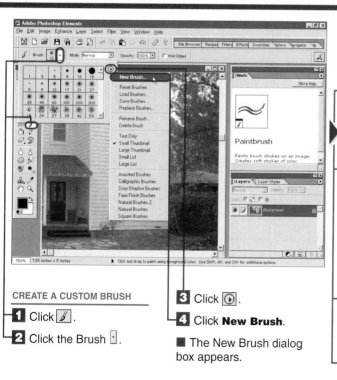

CREATE A CUSTOM BRUSH

1 Click 🖌.

2 Click the Brush ⊡.

3 Click ⊙.

4 Click **New Brush**.

■ The New Brush dialog box appears.

5 Click and drag the sliders (△) and type values to define the new brush attributes.

6 Type a name for the brush.

7 Click **OK**.

■ The new brush appears in the brush menu.

Note: To apply the brush, see the section "Using the Paintbrush Tool."

USING THE AIRBRUSH TOOL

You can use the Airbrush tool to add color to your image. The Airbrush applies a softer line than the paintbrush.

USING THE AIRBRUSH TOOL

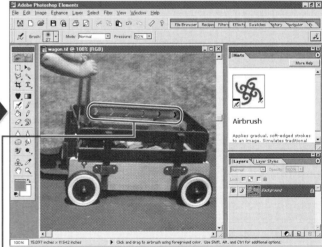

1 Click the Airbrush tool (■).

2 Click ■ to select a color with which to paint.

Note: For details, see the section "Select the Foreground and Background Colors."

3 Click the Brush ⊡ and select a brush size and type.

4 Click and drag ○ to apply the foreground color to the image.

■ To undo the most recent brush stroke, click **Edit** and then **Undo Airbrush**.

Note: To undo more than one brush stroke, see Chapter 2 to learn how to use the History palette.

What happens when I click and hold with the Airbrush tool?

Doing so causes a constant stream of color to come out of the tool, enlarging the painted area. The Airbrush tool is the only painting tool whose effects change the longer you apply it in one place.

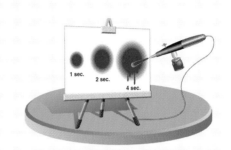

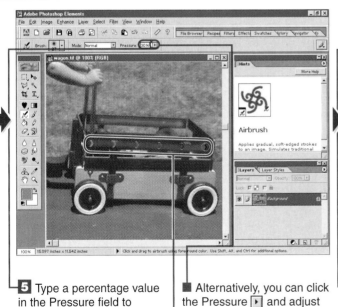

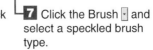

5 Type a percentage value in the Pressure field to change the opacity of the brush strokes.

■ Alternatively, you can click the Pressure ► and adjust the slider.

6 Click and drag ○ to apply the semitransparent airbrush.

7 Click the Brush · and select a speckled brush type.

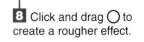

8 Click and drag ○ to create a rougher effect.

USING THE PAINT BUCKET TOOL

You can fill areas in your image with solid color using the Paint Bucket tool.

The Paint Bucket tool affects adjacent pixels in the image. You can set the Paint Bucket's Tolerance value to determine what range of colors the paint bucket affects in the image when you apply it.

To fill the pixels of a selected area rather than just adjacent pixels, see the section "Fill a Selection."

USING THE PAINT BUCKET TOOL

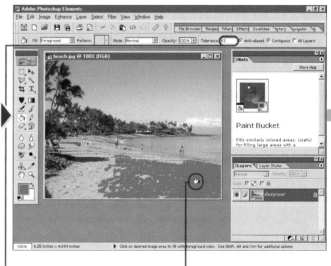

SELECT THE PAINT BUCKET TOOL

1 Click the Paint Bucket tool ( ).

2 Click ■ to select a color for painting.

Note: For details, see the section "Select the Foreground and Background Colors."

SET THE TOLERANCE

3 Type a Tolerance value from 0 to 255.

4 Click your cursor ( ) inside the image.

■ Elements fills an area of the image with the foreground color.

How can I reset a tool to the default settings?

Click on the tool's icon on the far left side of the Options bar and select **Reset Tool** from the menu that appears.

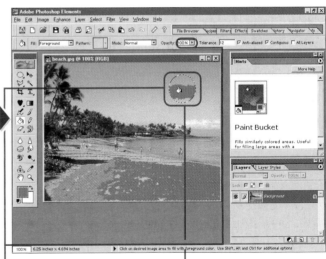

SET IMAGE OPACITY

5 To fill an area with a semitransparent color, type a percentage value of less than 100 in the Opacity field.

6 Click 🖑 inside the image.

■ Elements fills an area with see-through paint.

CONSTRAIN THE COLOR

7 To constrain where you apply the color, make a selection before clicking.

■ In this example, the Opacity was reset to 100%.

8 Click 🖑 inside the selection.

■ The fill effect stays within the boundary of the selection.

105

USING THE IMPRESSIONIST BRUSH

You can apply artistic styles to your image with the Impressionist Brush. The brush creates its effect by blending existing colors in an image together.

USING THE IMPRESSIONIST BRUSH

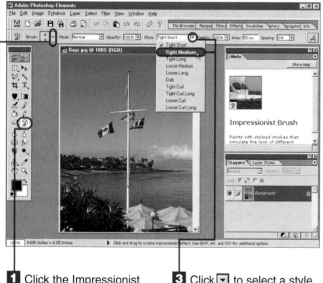

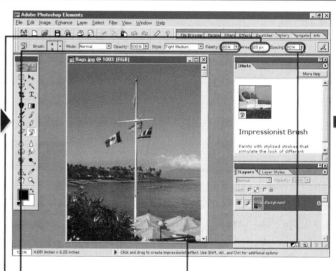

1 Click the Impressionist Brush tool ( ).

2 Click the Brush and select a brush size and type.

3 Click to select a style, which controls the shape of the brush.

4 Type a fidelity — from 0 to 100 — to determine how much the color deviates beneath the brush.

5 Type the area — from 0 to 500 — covered by the brush strokes.

6 Type a spacing from 0 to 100.

■ A high spacing limits the brush effects only to areas that differ considerably from the source.

How do I decrease the effects that I apply with the Impressionist Brush?

An easy way is to decrease the opacity of the brush. This way, Elements retains more of the original image's features.

7 Click and drag ◯ to apply the brush.

■ The colors blend to mimic the style of an impressionist painting.

■ You can change the settings to achieve a different effect.

■ Here, the style has been changed to Tight Curl.

■ You can click 🔄 to undo previously applied brush strokes.

USING THE CLONE STAMP

You can clean up small flaws or erase elements in your image with the Clone Stamp tool. The tool copies information from one area of an image to another.

USING THE CLONE STAMP

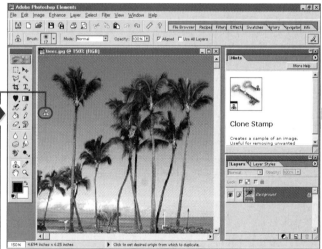

1 Click the Clone Stamp tool (🖳).

2 Click the Brush 🔽.

3 Select a brush size and type.

4 Press and hold Alt (option) and click the area of the image from which you want to copy.

■ This example uses the tool to select an area of sky.

How can I make the clone stamp's effects look seamless?

To erase elements from your image with the rubber stamp without leaving a trace, try the following:

- Clone between areas of similar color and texture.

- To apply the rubber stamp more subtly, lower its opacity.

- Use a soft-edged brush shape.

5 Release the Alt (option) key.

6 Click and drag ◯ inside the selection to apply the clone stamp.

■ Elements copies the selected area to where you click and drag.

7 Click and drag ◯ repeatedly over the image to achieve the desired effect.

■ As you apply the tool, you can press Alt (option) and click again to select a different area from which to copy.

■ This example uses a selection of the sky to cover a tree in the image.

USING THE PATTERN STAMP

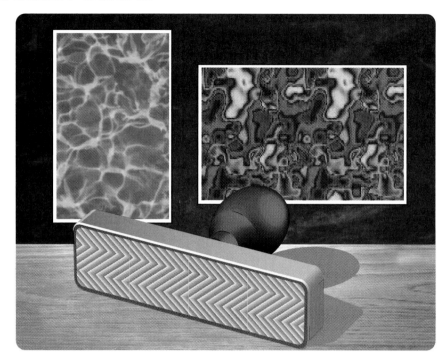

You can paint with a pattern using the Pattern Stamp tool. The tool gives you a free-form way to add repeating elements to your images.

USING THE PATTERN STAMP

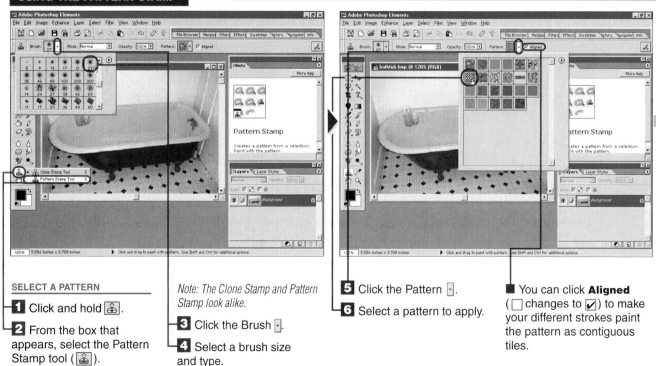

SELECT A PATTERN

1 Click and hold.

2 From the box that appears, select the Pattern Stamp tool.

Note: The Clone Stamp and Pattern Stamp look alike.

3 Click the Brush.

4 Select a brush size and type.

5 Click the Pattern.

6 Select a pattern to apply.

■ You can click **Aligned** (□ changes to ✔) to make your different strokes paint the pattern as contiguous tiles.

How do I define my own custom patterns?

Select what you want to use as a pattern in the image window with the Rectangular Marquee ([▢]), click **Edit,** and then click **Define Pattern.** A dialog box opens allowing you to name the new pattern. Clicking **OK** adds the new pattern to the Pattern menu. For more on the Rectangular Marquee and how to select objects, see Chapter 4.

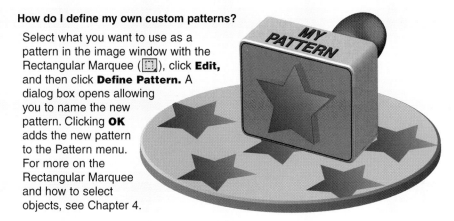

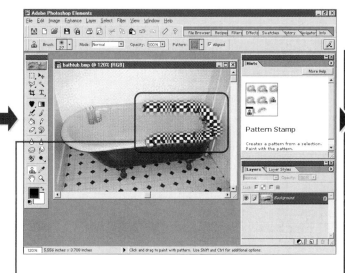

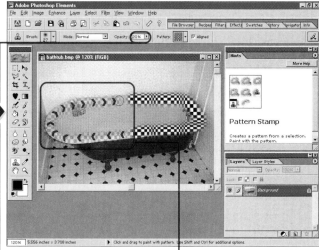

7 Click and drag ◯ inside the selection to apply the pattern.

■ The pattern applies to where you click and drag.

APPLY A DIFFERENT OPACITY

8 Type a value of less than 100 in the Opacity box.

9 Click and drag ◯ inside the selection to apply the pattern.

■ Decreasing the opacity applies a semi-transparent pattern.

FILL A SELECTION

You can fill a selection with the Fill command, an alternative to the Paint Bucket tool. The Fill command differs from the Paint Bucket tool in that it fills the entire selected area, not just adjacent pixels based on a tolerance value.

See the section "Using the Paint Bucket Tool" if you want to fill adjacent pixels rather than a selected area.

FILL A SELECTION

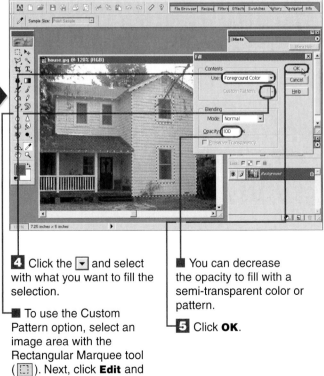

1 Define the area you want to fill using a selection tool.

Note: See Chapter 4 for more on using selection tools.

2 Click **Edit**.

3 Click **Fill**.

4 Click the ⏷ and select with what you want to fill the selection.

■ To use the Custom Pattern option, select an image area with the Rectangular Marquee tool (⬚). Next, click **Edit** and then **Define Pattern**.

■ You can decrease the opacity to fill with a semi-transparent color or pattern.

5 Click **OK**.

How do I apply a "ghosted" white layer over part of an image?

Use a selection tool to define the area of the image that you want to cover. Then apply the Fill command with White selected and the Opacity set to less than 50%.

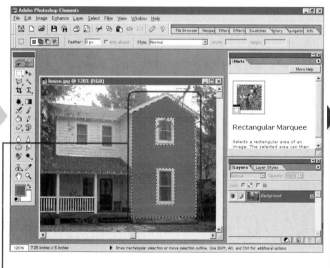

■ Elements fills the area.

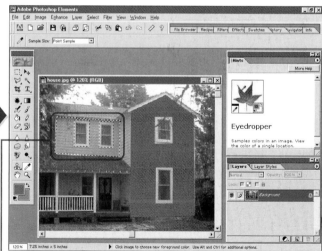

■ You can select other areas and fill them with different colors.

■ This example uses a fill with the background color set to 30% opacity.

STROKE A SELECTION

You can use the Stroke command to draw a line along the edge of a selection. This can help you highlight objects in your image.

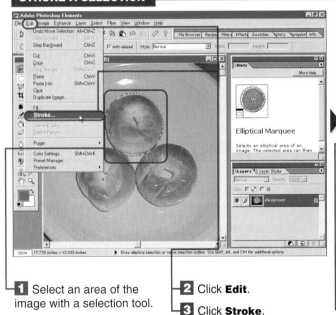

1 Select an area of the image with a selection tool.

Note: See Chapter 4 for more on using selection tools.

2 Click **Edit**.

3 Click **Stroke**.

■ The Stroke dialog box appears.

4 Type a width.

5 Click **Inside** to stroke a line on the inside of the selection, **Center** to stroke a line straddling the selection, or **Outside** to stroke a line on the outside of the selection (○ changes to ◉).

■ You can click the color box to define the color of the stroke.

6 Click **OK**.

How do I add a colored border to the outside of my image?

Click **Select** and then **All.** Then apply the Stroke command, clicking **Inside** as the Location. Elements adds a border to the image.

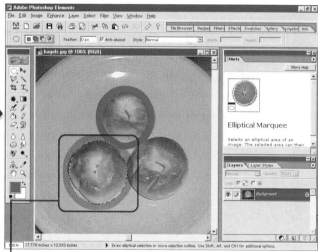

■ Elements strokes a line along the selection.

■ You can select other areas and stroke them using different settings.

■ This stroke was applied to the outside of the selection at 30% opacity.

DRAW A SHAPE

You can create solid shapes in your image using Elements' many shape tools.

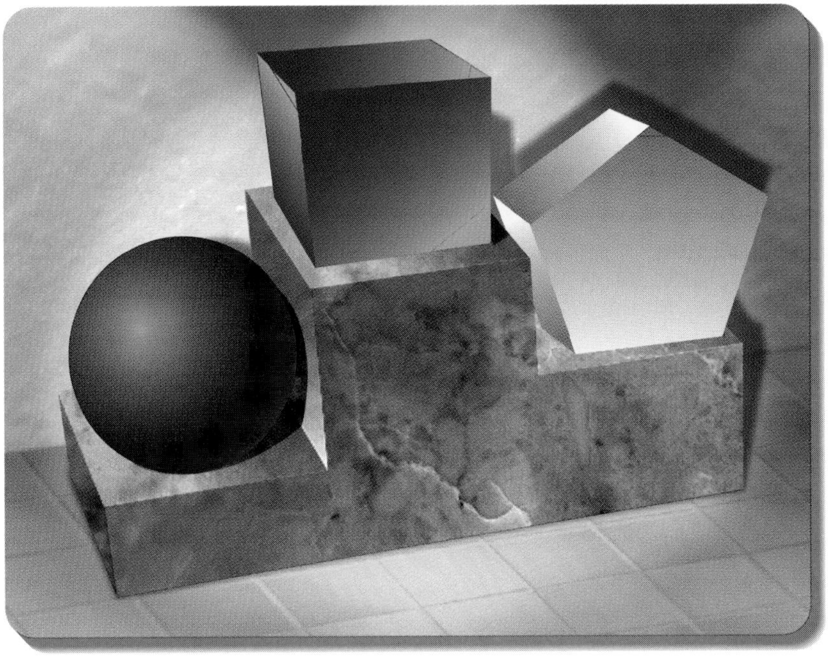

DRAW A SHAPE

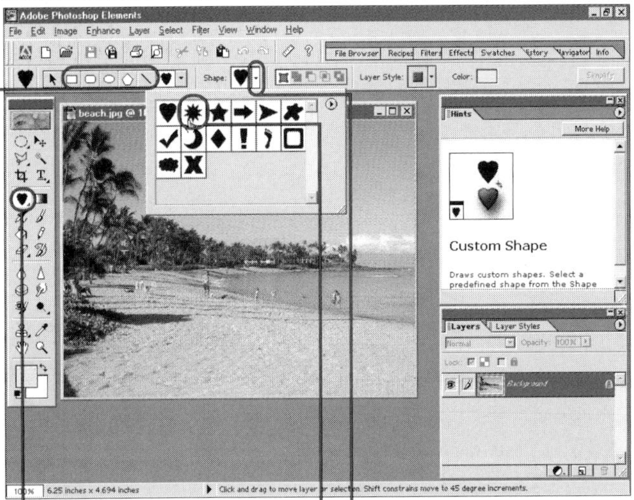

1 Click the Custom Shape tool (♥).

Note: The tool icon may differ, depending on what type of shape you drew last.

■ You can select from standard shapes in the Options bar.

2 Click the Shape ▾.

3 Click a shape.

4 Press **Enter** (**Return**) to close the menu.

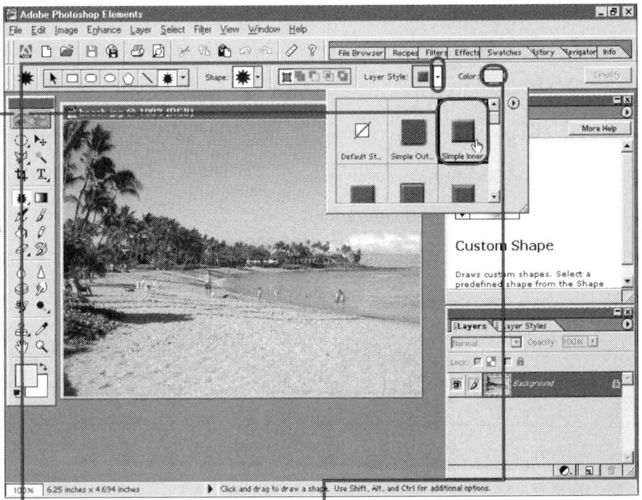

5 Click the Layer Style ▾.

6 Click a style for your shape.

■ Elements offers a variety of 3D styles.

7 Press **Enter** (**Return**) to close the menu.

■ You can click the Color box (□) to select a different shape color.

How do I resize a shape after I draw it?

Click the shape's layer and then click the Custom Shape tool (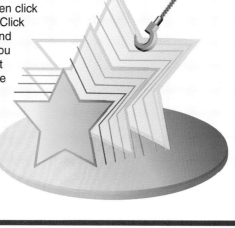). Click **Image, Transform Shape,** and then a transform command. You can then resize the shape just like you would a selection. See Chapter 5 for more details on manipulating your shapes.

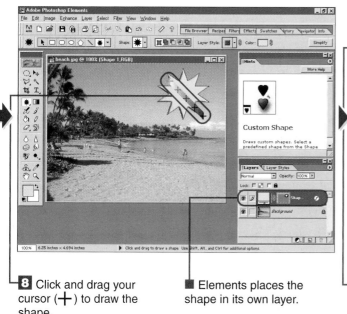

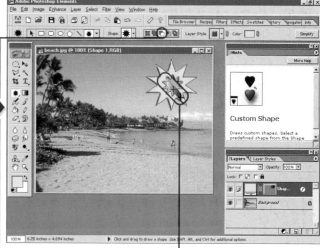

8 Click and drag your cursor (+) to draw the shape.

■ Elements places the shape in its own layer.

Note: For more about layers, see Chapter 8.

9 Click an overlay option.

■ In this example, Subtract from shape area is selected.

10 Click and drag + to draw another shape.

■ Elements applies your overlay option.

DRAW A LINE

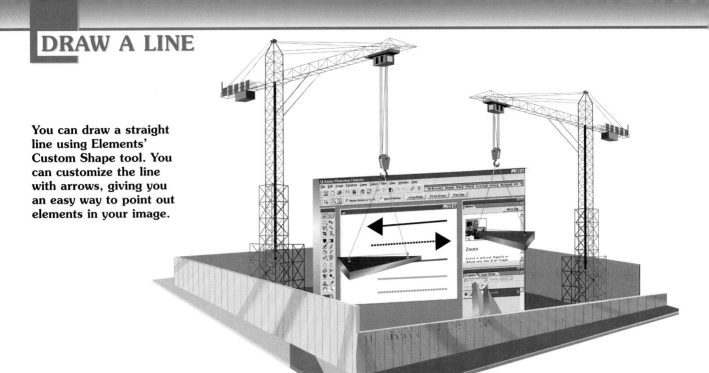

You can draw a straight line using Elements' Custom Shape tool. You can customize the line with arrows, giving you an easy way to point out elements in your image.

DRAW A LINE

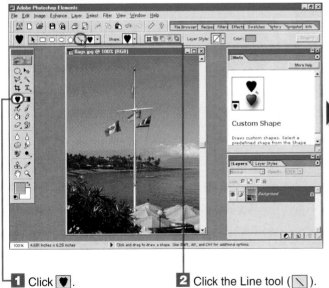

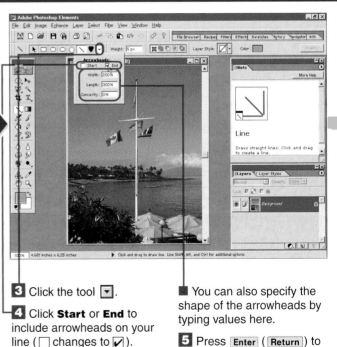

1 Click **♥**.

Note: The tool icon may differ, depending on what type of shape you drew last.

2 Click the Line tool (＼).

3 Click the tool ▼.

4 Click **Start** or **End** to include arrowheads on your line (□ changes to ☑).

■ You can also specify the shape of the arrowheads by typing values here.

5 Press **Enter** (**Return**) to close the menu.

118

How do I access more custom shapes?

Click the Custom Shape tool (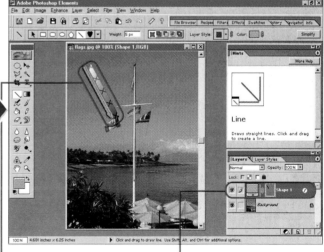), click ·, and then click ⓞ to open the menu. In the menu you can choose from different shape categories, including "Animals," "Office," and "Signs." Each category brings up a different set of shapes.

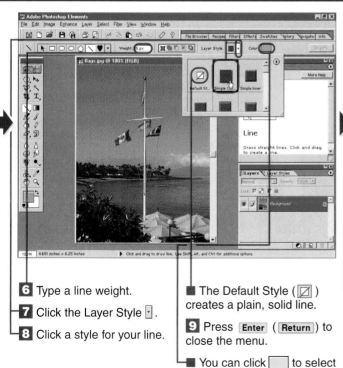

6 Type a line weight.

7 Click the Layer Style ·.

8 Click a style for your line.

■ The Default Style (▢) creates a plain, solid line.

9 Press Enter (Return) to close the menu.

■ You can click ▢ to select a different line color.

10 Click and drag ✛ to draw the line.

■ Elements places the line in its own layer.

Note: For more about layers, see Chapter 8.

APPLY A GRADIENT

You can apply a gradient, which is a blend from one color to another. This gives objects in your image a 3D look.

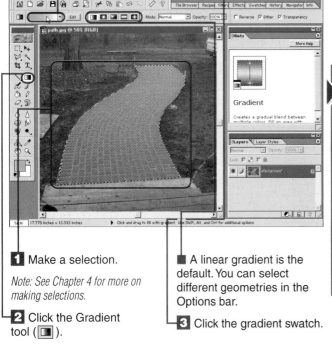  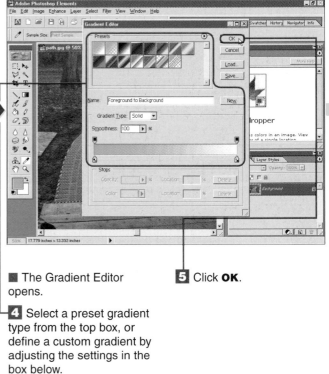

1 Make a selection.

Note: See Chapter 4 for more on making selections.

2 Click the Gradient tool (▣).

■ A linear gradient is the default. You can select different geometries in the Options bar.

3 Click the gradient swatch.

■ The Gradient Editor opens.

4 Select a preset gradient type from the top box, or define a custom gradient by adjusting the settings in the box below.

5 Click **OK**.

How can I add a rainbow gradient to my image?

Click a rainbow swatch in the Gradient Editor. Doing so applies the spectrum of colors from red to violet. For more about layers, see Chapter 8.

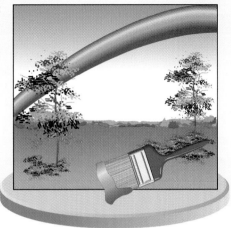

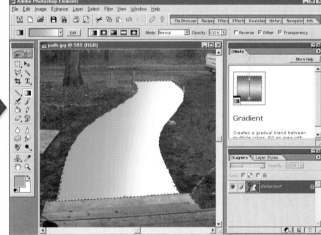

■ **6** Click and drag ✛ inside the selection.

■ This defines the direction and transition of the gradient.

■ Dragging a long line with the tool produces a gradual transition. Dragging a short line with the tool produces an abrupt transition.

■ Elements generates a gradient inside the selection.

CHAPTER 7

Adjusting Colors

Do you want to fine-tune the colors in your image — darken them, lighten them, or remove them completely? This chapter introduces the tools that let you do the trick.

CHANGE BRIGHTNESS AND CONTRAST

The Brightness/Contrast command provides a simple way to make adjustments to the highlights and shadows of your image.

To change the brightness or contrast of small parts of your image, use the Dodge and Burn tools. See "Using the Dodge and Burn Tools" in this chapter for details.

If you make a selection before performing the Brightness/Contrast command, changes only affect the selected pixels. Similarly, if you have a multilayered image, your adjustments only affect the selected layer. See Chapter 4 to make a selection and Chapter 8 for more on layers.

CHANGE BRIGHTNESS AND CONTRAST

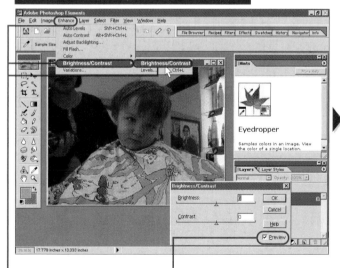

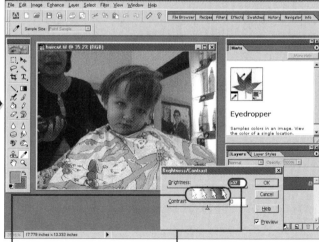

1 Click **Enhance**.

2 Click **Brightness/Contrast**.

3 Click **Brightness/Contrast**.

■ A dialog box opens with sliders set to 0.

4 To have your adjustments display in the image window as you make them, click **Preview** (☐ changes to ☑).

5 Click and drag the Brightness slider (△).

■ Drag the slider (△) to the right to lighten the image, or to the left to darken the image.

■ You can also lighten the image by typing a number from 1 to 100, or darken the image by typing a negative number from −1 to −100.

How can I adjust the contrast of an image automatically?

Click **Enhance,** and then **Auto Contrast.** Elements converts the very lightest pixels in the image to white and the very darkest pixels in the image to black. Making the highlights brighter and the shadows darker boosts the contrast, which can improve the appearance of poorly exposed photographs.

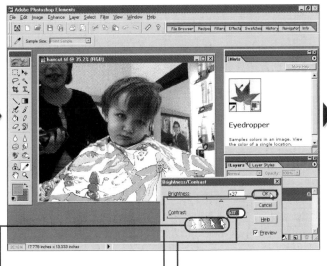

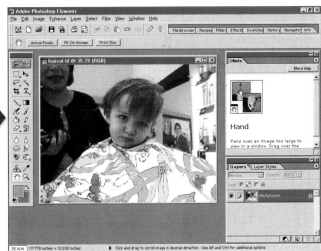

6 Click and drag the Contrast slider (△).

■ Drag △ to the right to increase the contrast, or to the left to decrease the contrast.

■ You can also increase the contrast by typing a number from 1 to 100, or decrease the contrast by typing a negative number from –1 to –100.

7 Click **OK**.

■ Elements applies the new brightness and contrast values.

USING THE DODGE AND BURN TOOLS

You can use the Dodge and Burn tools to brighten or darken a specific area of an image, respectively.

Dodge is a photographic term that describes the diffusing of light when developing a film negative. *Burn* is a photographic term that describes the focusing of light when developing a film negative.

These tools are an alternative to the Brightness/Contrast command, which affects the entire image. To brighten or darken the entire image, see the section "Change Brightness and Contrast."

USING THE DODGE TOOL

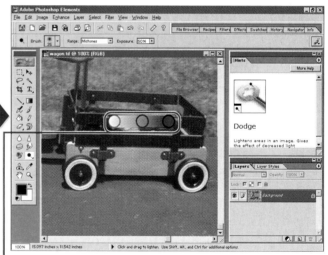

1 Click the Dodge tool ( ).

2 Click the Brush .

3 Click the brush size and style that you want to use.

■ You can also select the range of colors you want to affect and the tool's exposure, or strength.

4 Click and drag your cursor (○) over the area that you want to lighten.

■ Elements lightens the area.

How do I invert the bright and dark colors in an image?

Click **Image, Adjustments,** and then **Invert.** This makes the image look like a film negative. Bright colors become dark, and vice versa.

USING THE BURN TOOL

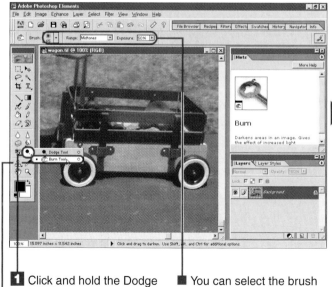

1 Click and hold the Dodge tool (⚫).

2 Click the Burn tool (✋) in the box that appears.

■ You can select the brush size and shape, the range of colors you want to affect, and the tool's exposure, or strength.

3 Click and drag ○ over the area that you want to darken.

■ Elements darkens the area.

USING THE BLUR AND SHARPEN TOOLS

You can sharpen or blur specific areas of your image with the Sharpen and Blur tools. This allows you to emphasize or de-emphasize objects in a photo.

You can blur or sharpen the entire image by using one of the Blur or Sharpen commands located in Elements' Filter menu. See Chapter 10 for more information.

USING THE BLUR TOOL

1 Click the Blur tool (△).

2 Click the Brush ⋅.

3 Click the brush size and shape that you want to use.

■ To change the pressure, or strength, of the tool, type a value from 1% to 100%.

4 Click and drag ○ to blur an area of the image.

What is the Smudge tool?

The Smudge tool () is another option in the Elements toolbox. It simulates dragging a finger through wet paint, shifting colors, and blurring your image.

USING THE SHARPEN TOOL

1 Click the Sharpen tool (△).

2 Click the Brush ⬝ and click the brush size and shape that you want to use.

■ Type a value from 1% to 100% to set the pressure, or strength, of the tool.

3 Click and drag ○ to sharpen an area of the image.

ADJUST LEVELS

The Levels command lets you make fine adjustments to the highlights, midtones, or shadows of an image.

Although more difficult to use, the Levels command offers more control over brightness than the Brightness/Contrast command covered in the section "Change Brightness and Contrast."

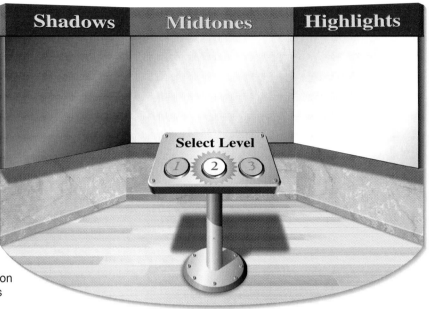

To affect only selected pixels, select them before performing the Levels command. Similarly, if you have a multilayered image, your adjustments only affect the selected layer. See Chapter 4 to make a selection and Chapter 8 for more on layers.

ADJUST LEVELS

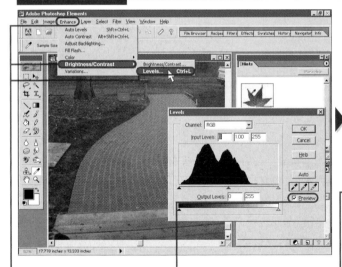

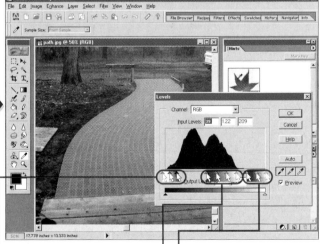

1 Click **Enhance**.

2 Click **Brightness/Contrast**.

3 Click **Levels**.

■ The Levels dialog box appears.

4 To display your adjustments in the image window as you make them, click **Preview** (□ changes to ☑).

■ Use the Input sliders (△) to adjust an image's brightness, midtones, and highlights.

5 Click and drag ▲ to the right to darken shadows and increase contrast.

6 Click and drag △ to the left to lighten the bright areas of the image and increase contrast.

7 Click and drag ▲ to adjust the midtones of the image.

How do you adjust the brightness levels of an image automatically?

Click **Enhance** and then **Auto Levels.** Elements converts the very lightest pixels in the image to white and the very darkest pixels in the image to black. This command is similar to the Auto Contrast command and can quickly improve the contrast of an overly gray photographic image. See the section "Change Brightness and Contrast" for related information.

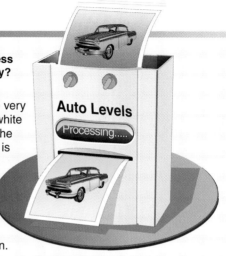

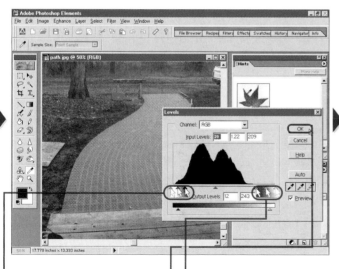

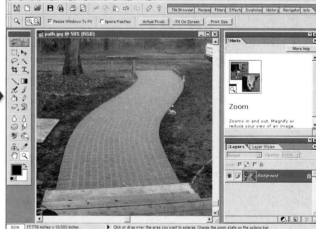

■ The Output sliders ◢ let you decrease the contrast while either lightening or darkening the image.

8 Click and drag ◢ to the right to lighten the image.

9 Click and drag ◢ to the left to darken the image.

10 Click **OK**.

■ Elements makes brightness and contrast adjustments to the image.

ADJUST HUE AND SATURATION

You can change the hue to shift the component colors of an image. You can change the saturation to adjust the color intensity in an image.

If you make a selection before performing the Hue/Saturation command, you only affect the selected pixels. Similarly, if you have a multilayered image, your adjustments only affect the selected layer. See Chapter 4 to make a selection and Chapter 8 for more on layers.

ADJUST HUE AND SATURATION

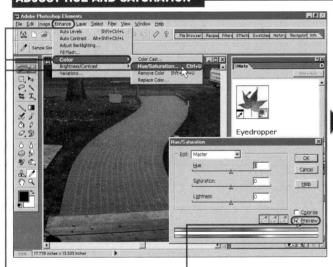

1 Click **Enhance**.

2 Click **Color**.

3 Click **Hue/Saturation**.

■ The Hue/Saturation dialog box appears.

4 To display your adjustments in the image window as you make them, click **Preview** (☐ changes to ☑).

5 Click and drag the Hue slider (△) to shift the colors in the image.

■ Dragging △ left or right shifts the colors in different, and sometimes bizarre ways.

■ In this example, adjusting the hue has changed the red to yellow.

How does the adjustment of an image's hues work?

When you adjust an image's hues in Elements, its colors shift according to their position on the color wheel. The color wheel is a graphical way of presenting all the colors in the visible spectrum.

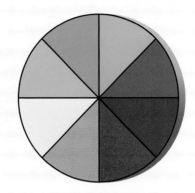

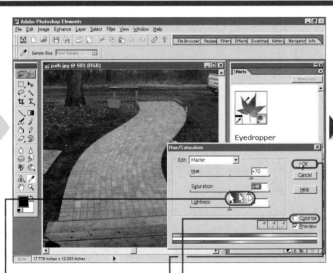

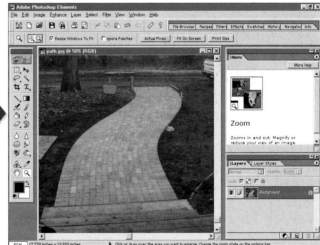

6 Click and drag the Saturation slider (△).

■ Dragging △ to the right or to the left increases or decreases the intensity of the image's colors, respectively.

■ Clicking **Colorize** (☐ changes to ☑), turns the image — even a grayscale one — into a monotone, or one-color, image. You can adjust the color with the sliders.

7 Click **OK**.

■ Elements makes the color adjustments to the image.

USING THE VARIATIONS COMMAND

The Variations command gives you a user-friendly interface with which to perform color adjustments in your image.

If you make a selection before performing the Variations command, you only affect the selected pixels. Similarly, if you have a multilayered image, your adjustments only affect the selected layer. See Chapter 4 to make a selection and Chapter 8 for more on layers.

USING THE VARIATIONS COMMAND

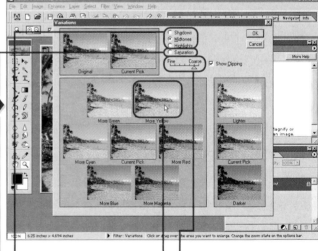

1 Click **Enhance**.

2 Click **Variations**.

■ The Variations dialog box appears.

3 Select a tonal range to apply effects to the different tones of your image (○ changes to ◉).

■ Alternatively, you can click **Saturation** (○ changes to ◉).

4 Click and drag △ left to make small adjustments or right to make large adjustments.

5 To add a color to your image, click one of the More thumbnails.

How can I undo color adjustments while using the Variations dialog box?

If you clicked one of the More thumbnail images to increase a color, you can click the More thumbnail image opposite to undo the effect. When you add colors in equal amounts to an image, the colors opposite one another — for example, red and cyan — cancel each other out. Note that clicking the **Original** image in the upper-left corner returns the image to its original state as well.

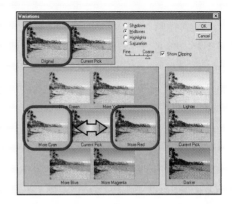

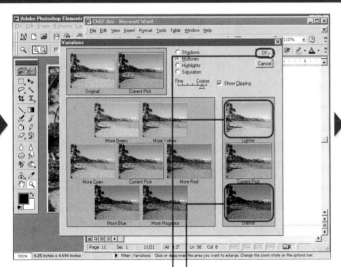

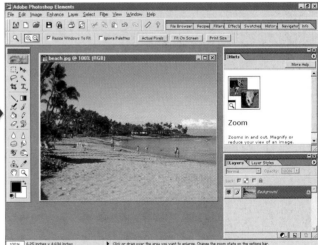

■ The result of the adjustment shows up in the Current Pick thumbnail.

■ To increase the effect, you can click the More thumbnail again.

■ You can decrease the brightness of the image by clicking **Darker**.

■ You can increase the brightness by clicking **Lighter**.

6 Click **OK**.

■ Elements makes the color adjustments to the image.

USING THE SPONGE TOOL

You can use the Sponge tool to adjust the color saturation, or color intensity, of a specific area of an image.

USING THE SPONGE TOOL

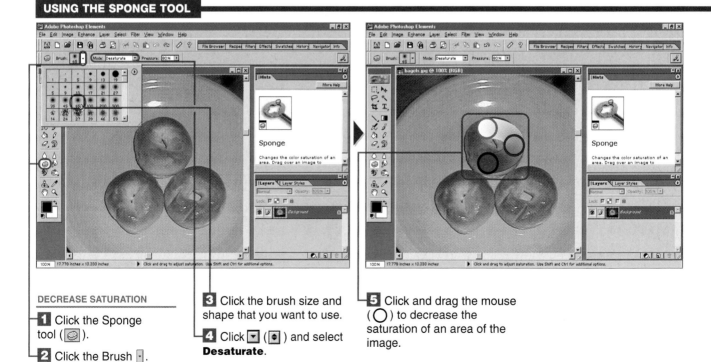

DECREASE SATURATION

1 Click the Sponge tool ().

2 Click the Brush ☐.

3 Click the brush size and shape that you want to use.

4 Click ☐ (☐) and select **Desaturate**.

5 Click and drag the mouse (○) to decrease the saturation of an area of the image.

How can I easily convert a color image to grayscale?

Click **Enhance, Color,** and then **Remove Color.** This command effectively sets the saturation value of the image to 0, converting it to grayscale.

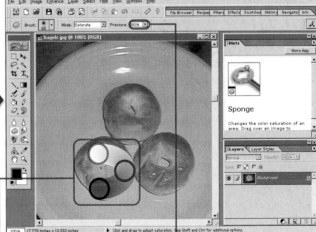

INCREASE SATURATION

1 Perform steps **1** through **3** on the previous page.

2 Click ▾ (♦) and select **Saturate**.

3 Click and drag ◯ to increase the saturation of an area of the image.

■ You can adjust the strength of the Sponge tool by changing the Pressure setting from 1% to 100%.

USING THE RED EYE BRUSH

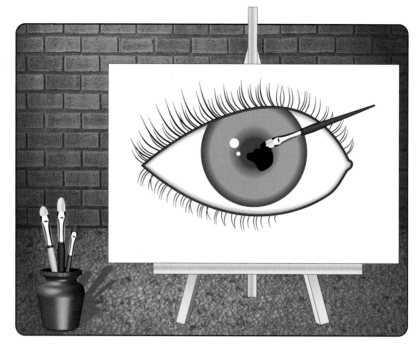

You can use the Red Eye Brush to remove the eye color that a camera flash can cause.

USING THE RED EYE BRUSH

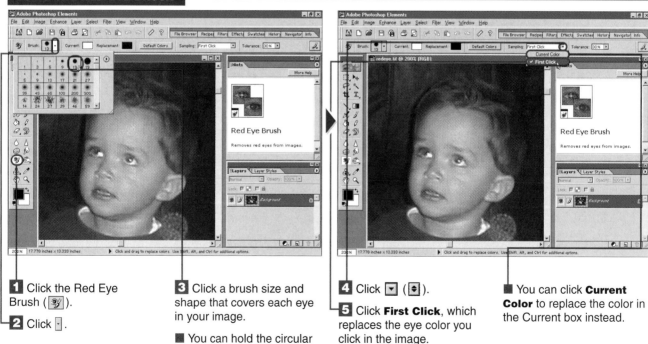

1 Click the Red Eye Brush (🖊).

2 Click ⋅.

3 Click a brush size and shape that covers each eye in your image.

■ You can hold the circular brush over an eye to match the brush to the eye size.

4 Click ▾ (⬍).

5 Click **First Click**, which replaces the eye color you click in the image.

■ You can click **Current Color** to replace the color in the Current box instead.

138

Why might I want to choose colors for the Red Eye Brush other than the default colors?

For eyes, the default settings will probably suffice. But if you use the brush to fix other elements in your image, you may want to adjust the colors. For example, you may want to specify the replacement color as white when getting rid of braces on teeth.

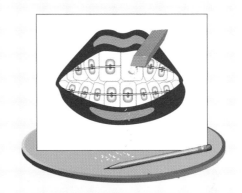

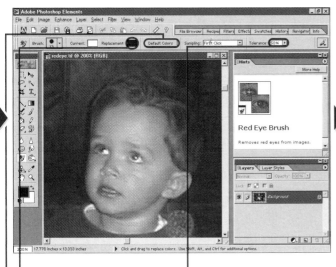

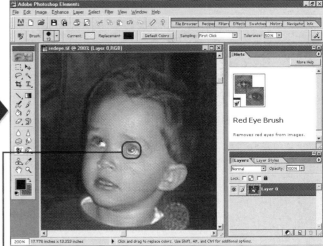

■ You can click the Replacement box (▇) to specify a replacement color other than black, the default.

■ You can click **Default Colors** to reset the Current and Replacement colors to red and black.

6 Type a tolerance from 1 to 100.

■ The higher the tolerance, the more red the brush removes.

7 Click a red eye.

■ Elements replaces the red with the replacement color.

ADJUST BACKLIGHTING

You can adjust the backlighting in an image to reduce the brightness caused by sun in the background and bring out some of the background details.

1 Click **Enhance**.

2 Click **Adjust Backlighting**.

■ The Adjust Backlighting dialog box appears.

3 Click and drag the Darker slider (△) to darken the backlighting.

4 Click **OK**.

■ Elements decreases the backlighting.

■ To make more precise lighting adjustments, you can use the Levels command as presented in the section "Adjust Levels."

ADD FILL FLASH

You can lighten the
shadows in a photo
using the Fill Flash
command. This can
help bring out details
that might otherwise
be hidden.

ADD FILL FLASH

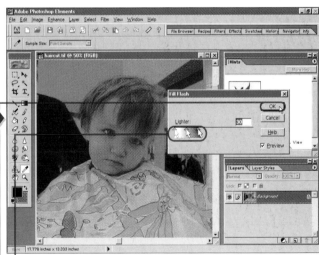

1 Click **Enhance**.

2 Click **Fill Flash**.

■ The Fill Flash dialog box
appears.

3 Click and drag the
Lighter slider (◢) to lighten
the image.

4 Click **OK**.

■ Elements lightens the
image.

■ To make more precise
lighting adjustments, use
the Levels command as
covered in the section
"Adjust Levels."

REPLACE A COLOR

The Replace Color command lets you select one or more colors in your image and then change them using hue, saturation, and lightness controls.

If you make a selection before performing the Replace Color command, you only affect the selected pixels. Similarly, if you have a multilayered image, your adjustments only affect the selected layer. See Chapter 4 to make a selection and Chapter 8 for more on layers.

REPLACE A COLOR

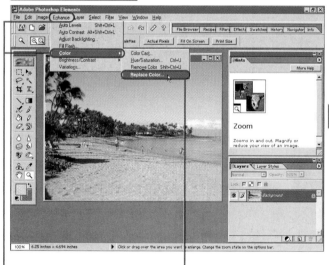

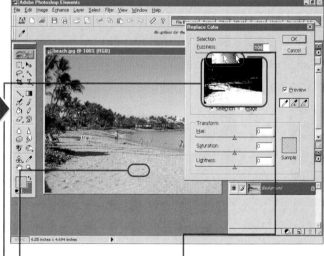

1 Click **Enhance**.

2 Click **Color**.

3 Click **Replace Color**.

■ The Replace Color dialog box appears.

4 Click in the image to select an area of color.

■ The selected area appears as white in the Selection preview.

5 Click and drag △ to specify the fuzziness.

■ Dragging to the right selects more color.

■ Dragging to the left selects less color.

How can I replace more than one area of color?

You can press `Shift` and then click inside your image to add areas of color to your selection. The white area inside the Selection box increases as you click. To deselect pixels from your selection, press `Alt` and then click (`option` and then click) a color inside your image.

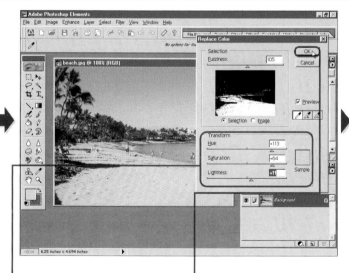

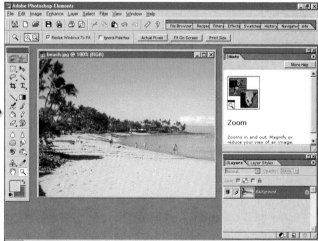

6 Click and drag the transform sliders (▲) to change the colors inside the selected area.

Note: For details about these controls, see the section "Adjust the Hue and Saturation."

7 Click **OK**.

■ Elements replaces the selected color.

REMOVE A COLOR CAST

You can use the Color Cast command to remove shading affecting your entire image. This command can help remove colors introduced by scanning.

If you make a selection before performing the Color Cast command, you only affect the selected pixels. Similarly, if you have a multilayered image, your adjustments only affect the selected layer. See Chapter 4 to make a selection and Chapter 8 for more on layers.

REMOVE A COLOR CAST

1 Click **Enhance**.

2 Click **Color**.

3 Click **Color Cast**.

■ The Color Cast Correction dialog box opens.

4 Click a part of your image that you want to make white, gray, or black.

■ Elements removes the color cast across the entire image.

■ You can click **Reset** to undo the command and try again.

5 Click **OK**.

■ Elements applies the change.

EQUALIZE COLORS

You can use the Equalize command to redistribute the brightness values in your image. This can lighten an overly dark or gray photo.

Elements equalizes an image by finding the lightest and darkest colors in the image and converting them to white and black. It also redistributes the colors in between.

If you make a selection before performing the command, Elements asks whether you want to equalize only the selection or equalize the entire image based on the selection.

EQUALIZE COLORS

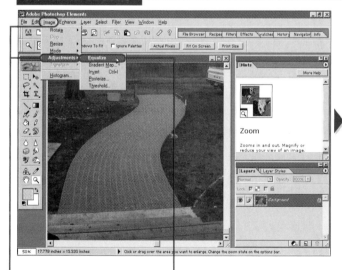

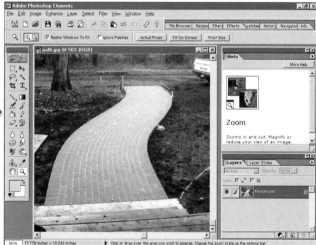

1 Click **Image**.

2 Click **Adjustments**.

3 Click **Equalize**.

■ Elements equalizes the colors in the image.

POSTERIZE COLORS

You can reduce the number of colors in your image using the Posterize command, which can give a photographic image a solid-color poster look.

If you make a selection before performing the Posterize command, you only affect the selected pixels. Similarly, if you have a multilayered image, your adjustments only affect the selected layer. See Chapter 4 to make a selection and Chapter 8 for more on layers.

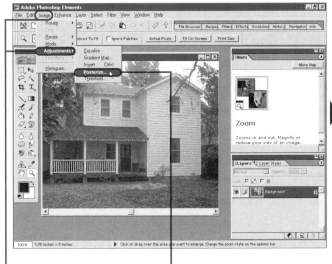

1 Click **Image**.

2 Click **Adjustments**.

3 Click **Posterize**.

■ The Posterize dialog box appears.

4 Type the number of levels.

■ More levels mean more solid colors.

■ Elements posterizes the image.

5 Click **OK**.

■ Elements applies the changes.

You can use the Threshold command to convert color or grayscale images into black-and-white images. Colors convert to either black or white depending on the threshold you set.

If you make a selection before performing the Threshold command, you only affect the selected pixels. Similarly, if you have a multilayered image, your adjustments only affect the selected layer. See Chapter 4 to make a selection and Chapter 8 for more on layers.

USING THE THRESHOLD COMMAND

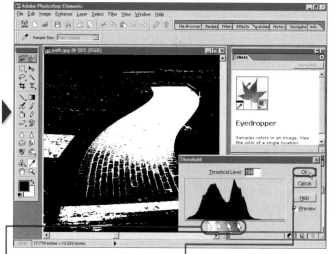

1 Click **Image**.

2 Click **Adjustments**.

3 Click **Threshold**.

4 Click and drag the slider (▲) to set a threshold between 1 and 255.

■ Elements converts the image to black and white colors.

5 Click **OK**.

■ Elements applies the changes.

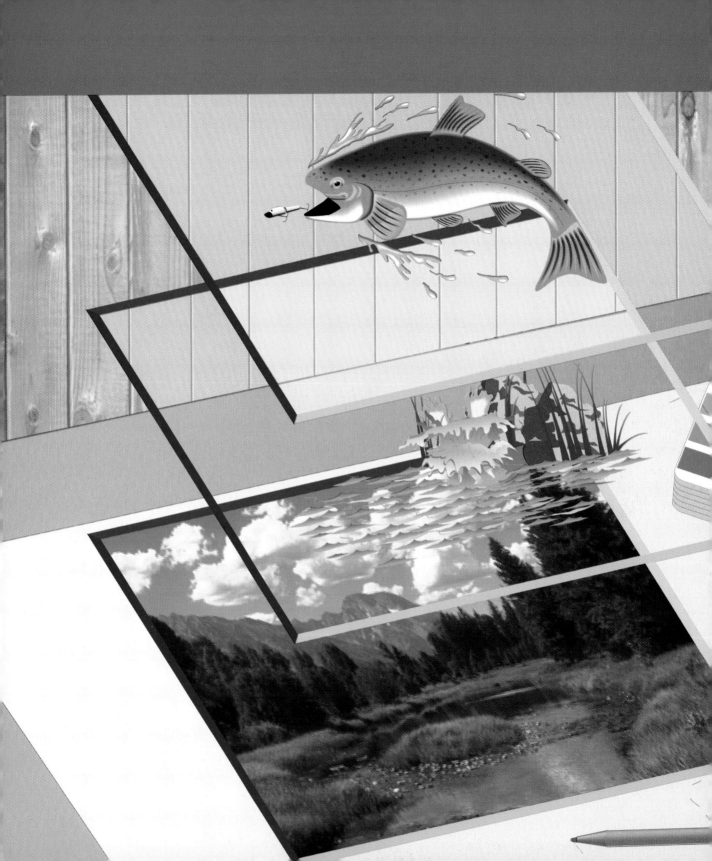

CHAPTER 8

Working with Layers

Do you want to separate the elements in your image so that you can move and transform them independently of one another? You can do this by placing them in different layers.

WHAT ARE LAYERS?

A Photoshop Elements image can consist of multiple layers, with each layer containing different objects in the image.

Layer Independence

Layered Elements files act like several images combined into one. Each layer of an image has its own set of pixels that you can move and transform independently of the pixels in other layers.

Apply Commands to Layers

Most Elements commands affect only the layer that you select. For example, if you click and drag using the Move tool, the selected layer moves while the other layers stay in place; if you apply a color adjustment, only colors in the selected layer change.

Manipulate Layers

You can combine, duplicate, and hide layers in an image. You can also shuffle the order in which you stack layers.

Transparency

Layers can have transparent areas where the elements on the layers below can show through. When you perform a cut or erase command on a layer, the affected pixels become transparent.

Adjustment Layers

Adjustment layers are special layers that contain information about color or tonal adjustments. An adjustment layer affects the pixels in all the layers below it. You can increase or decrease an adjustment layer's strength to get precisely the effect you want.

Save Layered Files

You can only save multilayered images in the Photoshop file format. To save a layered image in another file format — for example, PICT, TIFF, GIF, or JPEG — you must combine the image's layers into a single layer, a process known as *flattening*. For more information about saving files, see Chapter 13.

CREATE AND ADD TO A LAYER

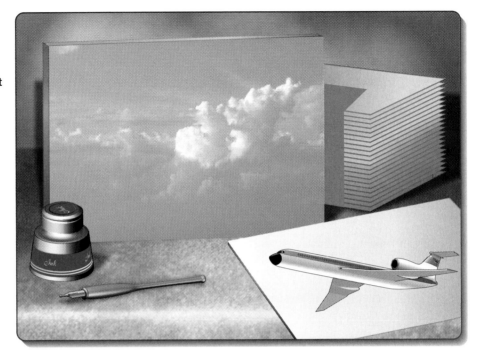

To keep elements in your image independent from one another, you can create separate layers and add objects to them.

CREATE A LAYER

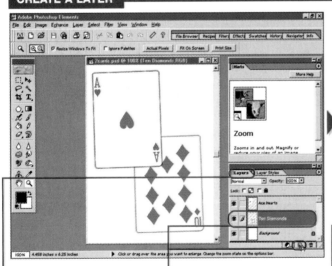

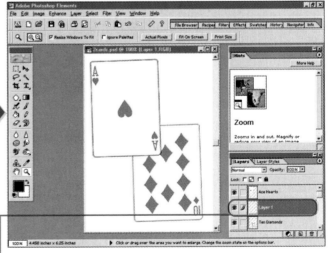

1 Click the **Layers** tab to select the Layers palette.

Note: For more information on opening and using palettes, see Chapter 1.

2 Click the layer above which you want to add the new layer.

3 In the Layers palette, click the New Layer button (⬜).

■ Alternatively, you can click **Layer**, **New**, and then **Layer**.

■ Elements creates a new, transparent layer.

Note: To change the name of a layer, see the section "Rename a Layer."

What is the Background layer?

The *Background layer* is the default bottom layer that appears when you create a new image or when you import an image from a scanner. You can create new layers on top of a Background layer, but not below it. Unlike other layers, a Background layer cannot contain transparent pixels.

ADD TO A LAYER

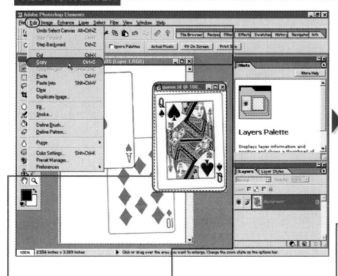

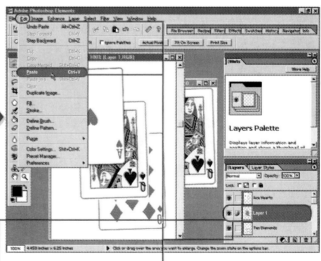

■ This example shows adding content to the new layer by copying and pasting from another image file.

1 Open another image.

2 Using a selection tool, select the content you want to copy from the other image.

Note: See Chapter 4 to learn more about the selection tools.

3 Click **Edit**.

4 Click **Copy**.

5 Click the image window where you created the new layer.

6 Click the new layer in the Layers palette.

7 Click **Edit**.

8 Click **Paste**.

■ The content from the other image pastes into the new layer.

HIDE A LAYER

You can hide a layer to temporarily remove elements in that layer from view.

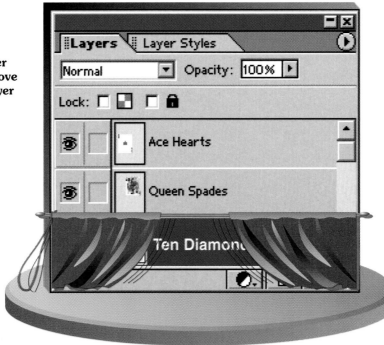

Hidden layers do not display when you print or use the Save for Web command.

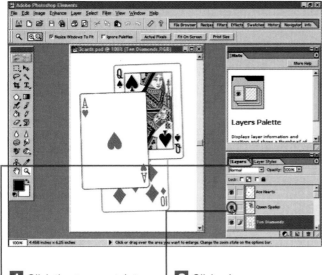

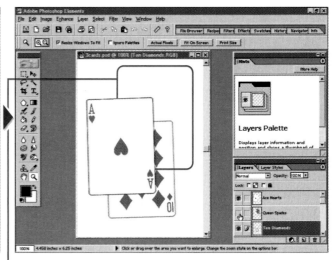

1 Click the **Layers** tab to select the Layers palette.

Note: For more about opening and using palettes, see Chapter 1.

2 Click a layer.

3 Click the Eye icon (👁) for the layer.

■ Elements hides the layer and 👁 disappears.

■ To show one layer and hide all the others, you can press Alt (option) and click the 👁 for the layer.

Note: You can also delete a layer. See the section "Delete a Layer" for more information.

154

You can use the Move
tool to reposition the
elements in one
layer without
moving those
in others.

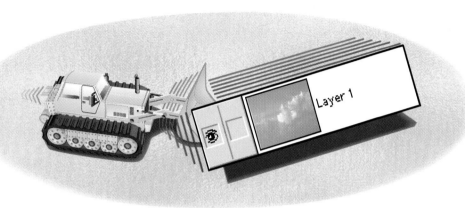

MOVE LAYER OBJECTS

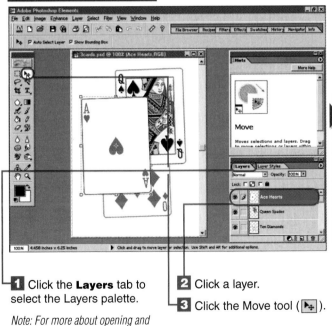

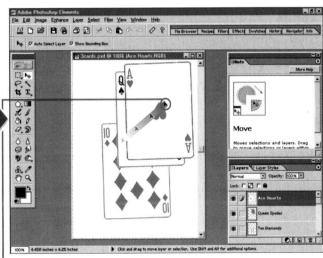

1 Click the **Layers** tab to
select the Layers palette.

*Note: For more about opening and
using palettes, see Chapter 1.*

2 Click a layer.

3 Click the Move tool ( ).

4 Click and drag your
cursor ( ) inside the
window.

■ Content in the selected
layer moves.

■ Content in the other layers
remains in the same
location.

*Note: To move several layers at
once, see the section "Link Layers."*

DUPLICATE A LAYER

By duplicating a layer, you can manipulate elements in an image while keeping a copy of their original state.

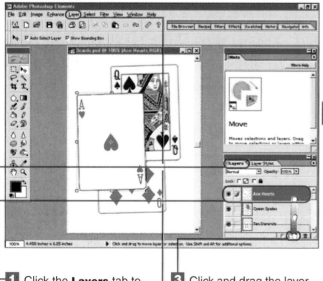
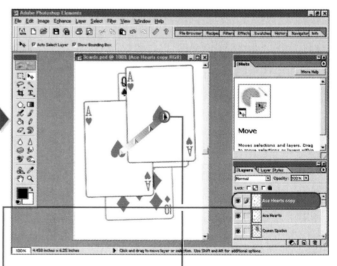

1 Click the **Layers** tab to select the Layers palette.

Note: For more about opening and using palettes, see Chapter 1.

2 Click a layer.

3 Click and drag the layer to 🔲.

■ Alternatively, you can click **Layer** and then **Duplicate Layer**, in which case a dialog box appears allowing you to name the layer.

■ Elements duplicates the selected layer.

■ You can see that Elements has duplicated the layer by selecting the new layer, clicking 🔁 and clicking and dragging the layer.

DELETE A LAYER

You can delete a layer
when you no longer have
a use for its contents.

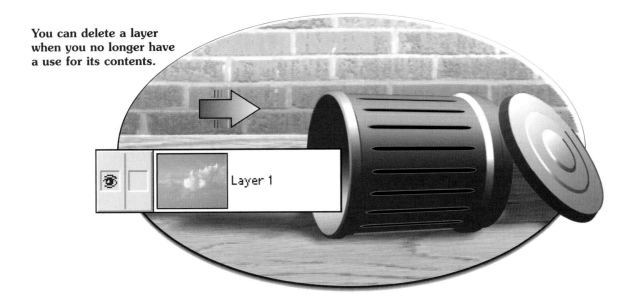

DELETE A LAYER

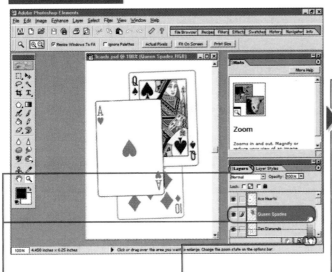

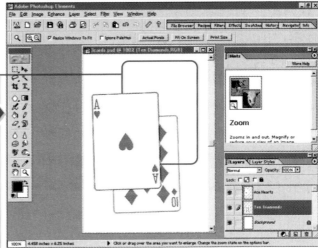

1 Click the **Layers** tab to
select the Layers palette.

*Note: For more about opening and
using palettes, see Chapter 1.*

2 Click a layer.

3 Click and drag the layer
to 🗑.

■ Alternatively, you can click
Layer and then **Delete
Layer**, in which case a
confirmation dialog box
appears.

■ Elements deletes the
selected layer and the content
in the layer disappears from
the image window.

*Note: You can also hide a layer. See
the section "Hide a Layer" for more
information.*

REORDER LAYERS

You can change
the stacking order
of layers to move
elements forward
or backward in
your image.

REORDER LAYERS

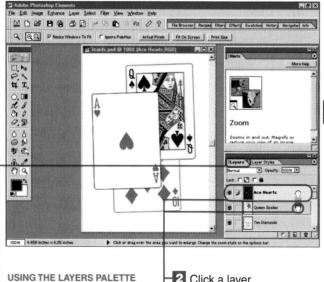

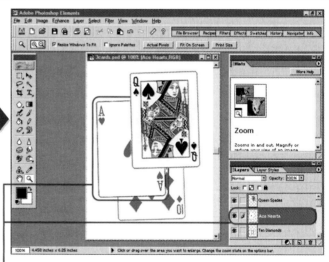

1 Click the **Layers** tab to
select the Layers palette.

*Note: For more about opening and
using palettes, see Chapter 1.*

2 Click a layer.

3 Click and drag the layer
to change its arrangement in
the stack.

■ The layer assumes its
new position in the stack.

**Are there shortcuts for
changing the order of layers?**

TO MOVE A LAYER	IN WINDOWS PRESS	ON A MAC PRESS
One level up in the stack	Ctrl +]	⌘ +]
One level back in the stack	Ctrl + [	⌘ + [
To the very front of a stack	Shift + Ctrl +]	Shift + ⌘ +]
To the very back of the stack	Shift + Ctrl + [	Shift + ⌘ + [

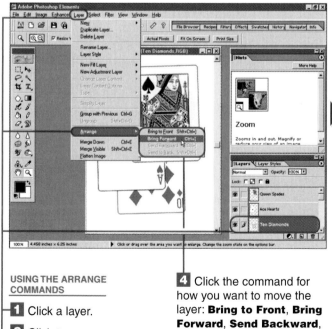

**USING THE ARRANGE
COMMANDS**

1 Click a layer.

2 Click **Layer**.

3 Click **Arrange**.

4 Click the command for
how you want to move the
layer: **Bring to Front**, **Bring
Forward**, **Send Backward**,
or **Send to Back**.

■ The layer assumes its
new position in the stack.

*Note: You cannot move a layer in
back of the default Background layer.*

CHANGE THE OPACITY OF A LAYER

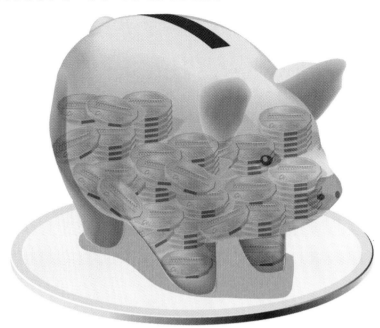

Adjusting the opacity of a layer can let elements in the layers below show through. *Opacity* is the opposite of transparency. Decreasing the opacity of a layer increases its transparency.

CHANGE THE OPACITY OF A LAYER

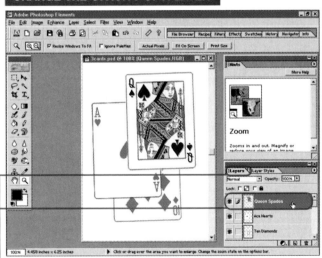

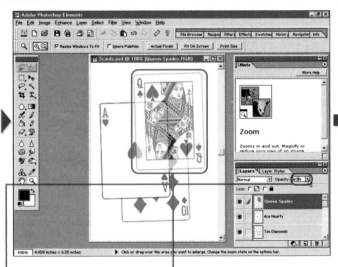

1 Click the **Layers** tab to select the Layers palette.

Note: For more about opening and using palettes, see Chapter 1.

2 Click a layer other than the Background layer.

Note: You cannot change the opacity of the Background layer.

■ The default opacity is 100%, which is completely opaque.

3 Type a new value in the Opacity field.

■ Alternatively, you can click ► and drag the slider.

■ A layer's opacity can range from 1% to 100%.

Note: To make a layer completely transparent, see the section "Hide a Layer."

■ The layer changes in opacity.

How can I use changes in opacity in my layers?

You can lower the opacity to add interesting type effects. For example, you can add a layer of semitransparent type over an image by reducing the type layer's opacity to 50%. For more about adding type, see Chapter 11.

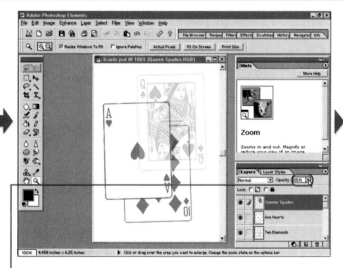

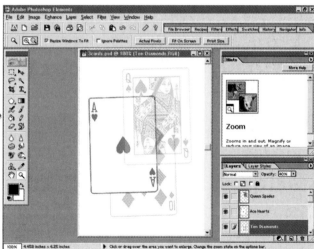

■ You can continue to adjust the opacity to suit your tastes.

■ You can make multiple layers in your image semitransparent by changing their opacities.

■ In this example, both the Queen Spades and Ten Diamonds layers are semitransparent.

MERGE AND FLATTEN LAYERS

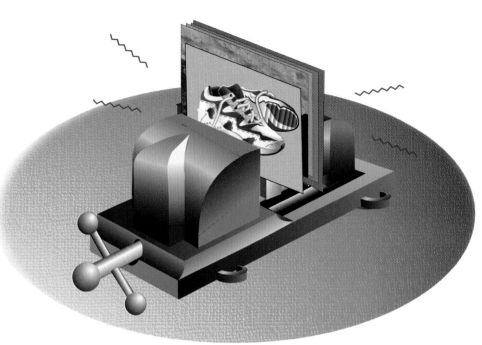

Merging layers lets
you permanently
combine information
from two or more
separate layers.
Flattening layers
combines all the
layers of an image
into one.

MERGE LAYERS

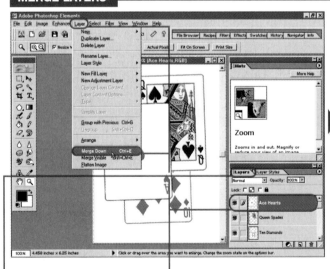

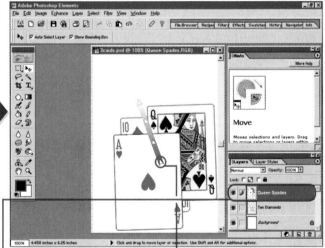

■1 Click the **Layers** tab to
select the Layers palette.

■2 Place the two layers you
want to merge next to each
other.

Note: To use palettes, see Chapter 1.
See the section "Reorder Layers" to
change stacking order.

■3 Click the topmost of the
two layers.

■4 Click **Layer**.

■5 Click **Merge Down**.

■ The two layers merge.

■ Elements keeps the
name of the lower layer.

■ To see the result of
the merge, select the new
layer, click ![move tool], and click and
drag the merged layer. The
elements that were previously
in separate layers now move
together.

Why would I want to merge layers?

Merging layers enables you to save computer memory. The fewer layers an Elements image has, the less space it takes up in RAM and on your hard drive when you save it. Merging layers also lets you permanently combine elements of your image when you are happy with how you have arranged them relative to one another. If you want the option of rearranging all the original layers in the future, save a copy of your image before you merge layers.

FLATTEN LAYERS

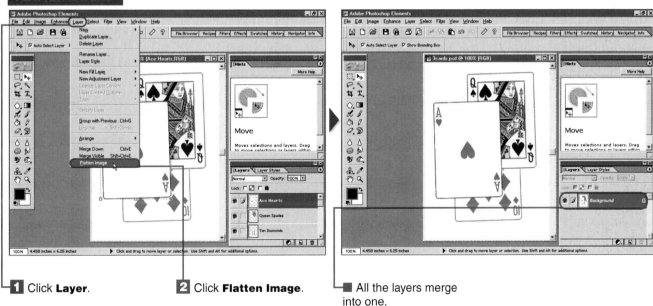

1 Click **Layer**.

2 Click **Flatten Image**.

■ All the layers merge into one.

RENAME A LAYER

You can rename a layer
to give it a name that
describes its content.

RENAME A LAYER

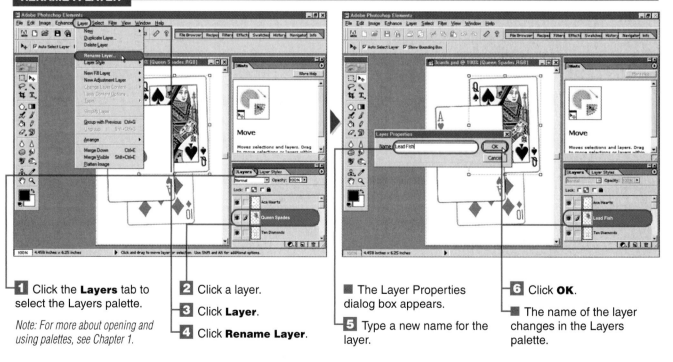

1 Click the **Layers** tab to
select the Layers palette.

*Note: For more about opening and
using palettes, see Chapter 1.*

2 Click a layer.

3 Click **Layer**.

4 Click **Rename Layer**.

■ The Layer Properties
dialog box appears.

5 Type a new name for the
layer.

6 Click **OK**.

■ The name of the layer
changes in the Layers
palette.

TRANSFORM A LAYER

You can use a transform tool to change the shape of the objects in a layer. Transforming a layer allows you to keep the rest of your image unchanged.

TRANSFORM A LAYER

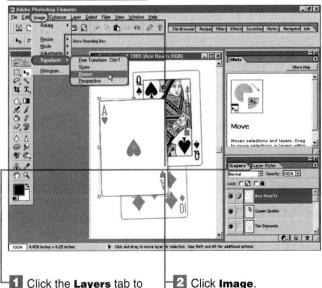

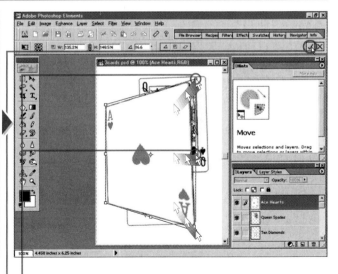

1 Click the **Layers** tab to select the Layers palette.

Note: For more about opening and using palettes, see Chapter 1.

2 Click **Image**.

3 Click **Transform**.

4 Click a transform tool.

5 Click and drag the side and corner handles to transform the shape of the layer.

6 Click ☑ or press **Enter** (**Return**) to commit the change.

■ You can click ☒ or press **Esc** (⌘ + .) to cancel the change.

Note: For more about transforming your images, see Chapter 5.

CREATE A SOLID FILL LAYER

You can create a solid
fill layer to place an
opaque layer of color
throughout your image.

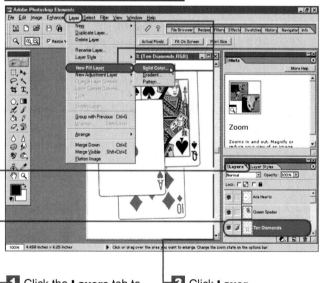

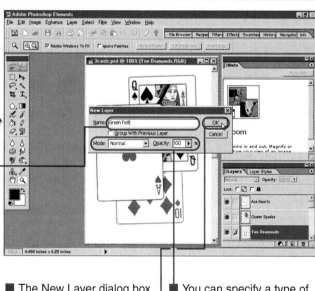

1 Click the **Layers** tab to
select the Layers palette.

*Note: For more about opening and
using palettes, see Chapter 1.*

2 Click the layer above
which you want to add
solid color.

3 Click **Layer**.

4 Click **New Fill Layer**.

5 Click **Solid Color**.

■ The New Layer dialog box
appears.

6 Type a name for the
layer.

■ You can specify a type of
blend or opacity setting for
the layer.

*Note: See "Blend Layers" or "Change
the Opacity of a Layer" for details.*

7 Click **OK**.

How do I add solid color to just part of a layer?

Make a selection with a selection tool before creating the solid fill layer. Elements only adds color inside the selection.

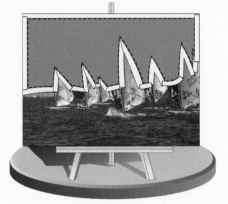

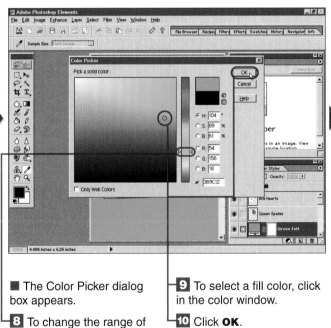

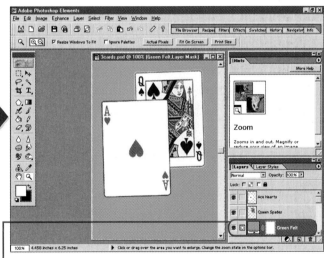

■ The Color Picker dialog box appears.

8 To change the range of colors that appears in the window, click and drag the slider (▷).

9 To select a fill color, click in the color window.

10 Click **OK**.

■ Elements creates a new layer filled with a solid color.

■ Layers above the new layer are not affected.

167

CREATE A GRADIENT FILL LAYER

You can create a
gradient fill layer to
place color transition
throughout your image.

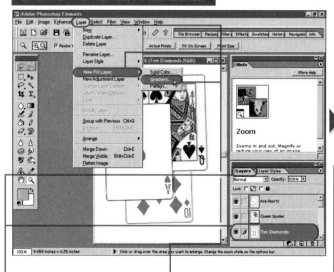

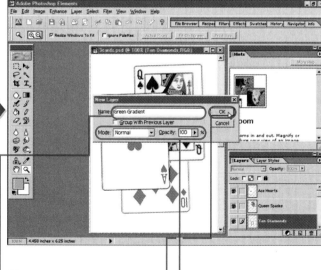

1 Click the **Layers** tab to select the Layers palette.

Note: For more about opening and using palettes, see Chapter 1.

2 Click the layer above which you want to add a gradient.

3 Click **Layer**.

4 Click **New Fill Layer**.

5 Click **Gradient**.

■ The New Layer dialog box appears.

6 Type a name for the layer.

■ You can specify a type of blend or opacity setting for the layer.

Note: See the section "Blend Layers" or "Change the Opacity of a Layer" for details.

7 Click **OK**.

Can I convert one type of fill layer to another?

Yes. First select the layer in the Layers palette. Then click **Layer, Change Layer Content,** and then a different layer type.

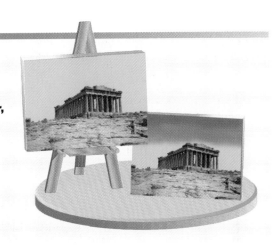

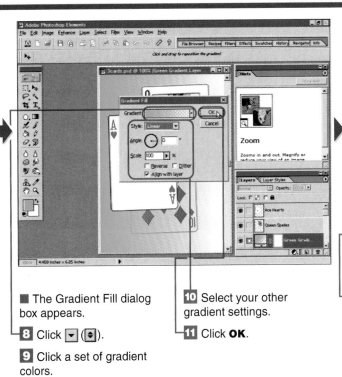

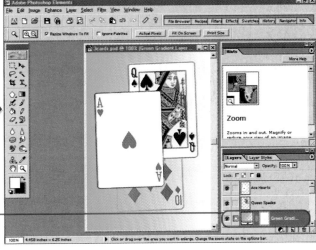

■ The Gradient Fill dialog box appears.

8 Click □ (⊟).

9 Click a set of gradient colors.

10 Select your other gradient settings.

11 Click **OK**.

■ Elements creates a new layer filled with a gradient.

■ Layers above the new layer remain unaffected.

CREATE A PATTERN FILL LAYER

You can create a pattern fill layer to place repeating designs throughout your image.

CREATE A PATTERN FILL LAYER

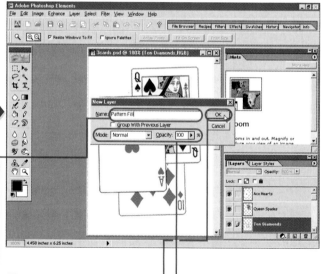

1 Click the **Layers** tab to select the Layers palette.

Note: For more about opening and using palettes, see Chapter 1.

2 Click the layer above which you want to add a pattern.

3 Click **Layer**.

4 Click **New Fill Layer**.

5 Click **Pattern**.

■ The New Layer dialog box appears.

6 Type a name for the layer.

■ You can specify a type of blend or opacity setting for the layer.

Note: See "Blend Layers" or "Change the Opacity of a Layer" for details.

7 Click **OK**.

How do I change the applied pattern after creating the layer?

Double-click the layer thumbnail in the Layers palette. The Pattern Fill dialog box appears and enables you to edit the pattern.

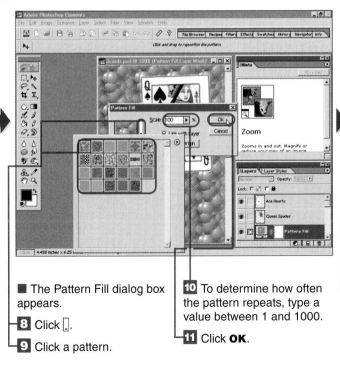

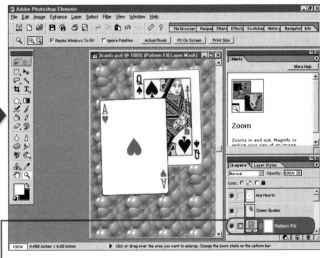

■ The Pattern Fill dialog box appears.

8 Click 🔽.

9 Click a pattern.

10 To determine how often the pattern repeats, type a value between 1 and 1000.

11 Click **OK**.

■ Elements creates a new layer filled with a pattern.

■ Layers above the new layer remain unaffected.

CREATE AN ADJUSTMENT LAYER

Adjustment layers let you store color and tonal changes in a layer, rather than having them permanently applied to your image.

Saturation = -10

CREATE AN ADJUSTMENT LAYER

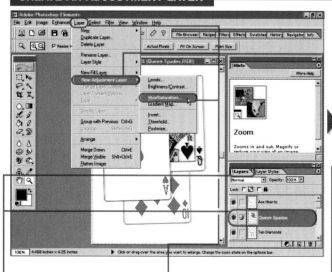

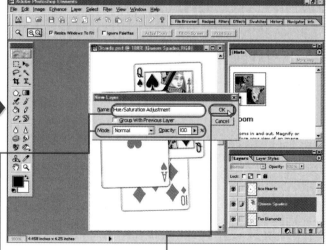

1 Click the **Layers** tab to select the Layers palette.

Note: For more about opening and using palettes, see Chapter 1.

2 Click a layer.

3 Click **Layer**.

4 Click **New Adjustment Layer**.

5 Click an adjustment command.

■ The New Layer dialog box appears.

6 Type a name for the adjustment layer.

■ You can specify a type of blend or opacity setting for the layer.

Note: See the section "Blend Layers" or "Change the Opacity of a Layer" for details.

7 Click **OK**.

■ Elements places the new adjustment layer above the currently selected layer.

How do I apply an adjustment layer to only part of my image canvas?

Make a selection with a selection tool before creating the adjustment layer. See Chapter 4 for more on selection tools.

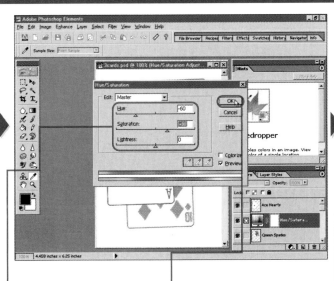

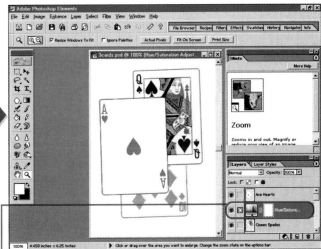

■ The dialog box for the adjustment command appears.

8 Click and drag the sliders (▲) and type values to adjust the settings.

■ In this example, an adjustment layer is created that changes the hue and saturation.

9 Click **OK**.

■ Elements adds an adjustment layer to the image.

■ Elements applies the effect to the layers that are below the adjustment layer.

■ In this example, Elements affects the card layers below the adjustment layer while leaving the card layer above it unaffected.

EDIT AN ADJUSTMENT LAYER

You can change the color and tonal changes that you defined in an adjustment layer. This lets you fine-tune your adjustment layer to get the effect you want.

EDIT AN ADJUSTMENT LAYER

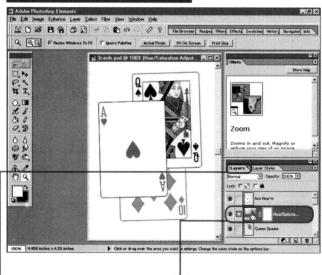

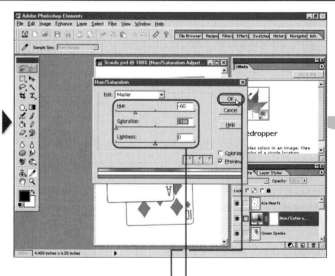

1 Click the **Layers** tab to select the Layers palette.

Note: For more about opening and using palettes, see Chapter 1.

2 Double-click the adjustment layer in the Layers palette.

■ The settings dialog box corresponding to the adjustment command appears.

3 Click and drag the sliders (△) to change the settings in the dialog box.

4 Click **OK**.

How do I merge an adjustment layer with a regular layer?

Place the adjustment layer above the layer with which you want to merge it and then click **Layer** and **Merge Down**. When you merge the layers, Elements only applies the adjustment layer's effects to the layer with which it is merged. The other layers below it remain unaffected.

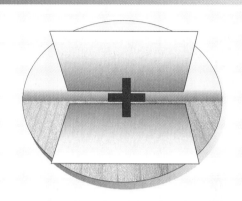

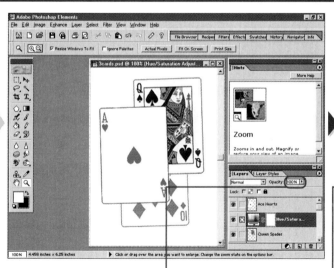

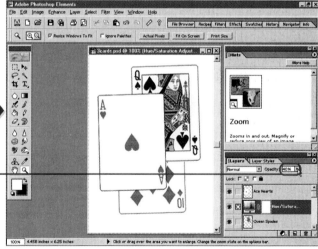

■ Elements applies your changes.

■ In this example, the saturation was reduced to the minimum, which removed the color in the layers below the adjustment layer.

■ You can lessen the affect of an adjustment layer by decreasing the layer's opacity to less than 100%.

■ In this example, the opacity was decreased to 40%, which reverses the decrease in saturation. Some of the original color in the cards returns.

LINK LAYERS

Linking causes different layers to move in unison when you move them with the Move tool. You may find linking useful when you want to keep elements of an image aligned with one another, but do not want to merge their layers. Keeping layers unmerged lets you apply effects independently of each. See the section "Merge and Flatten Layers" for more on merging.

LINK LAYERS

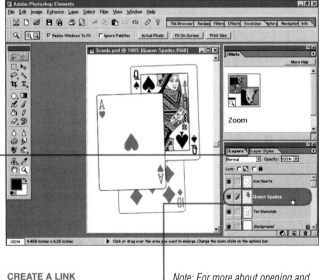
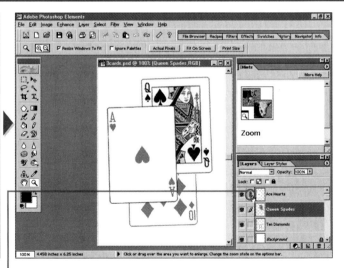

CREATE A LINK

1 Click the **Layers** tab to select the Layers palette.

Note: For more about opening and using palettes, see Chapter 1.

2 Click one of the layers you want to link.

3 Click the box next to the other layer that you want to link.

■ Doing so turns on a linking icon (📦).

■ The layers link together.

How do I keep from changing a layer after I have it the way I want it?

You can lock the layer by clicking the box to the left of the Lock icon (🔒) located on the Layers palette (☐ changes to ☑). You cannot move, delete, or otherwise edit a locked layer. You can click the box to the left of the Transparency icon (🔲) if you just want to prevent a user from editing the transparent pixels in the layer.

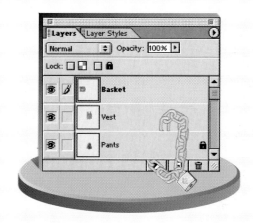

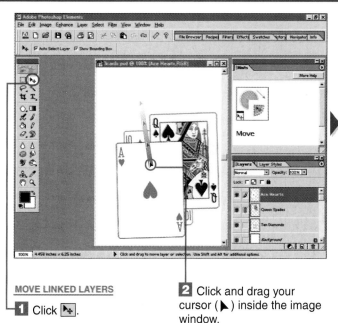

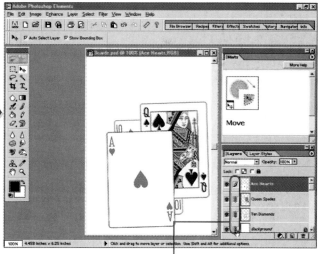

MOVE LINKED LAYERS

1 Click 🔤.

2 Click and drag your cursor (▶) inside the image window.

■ The linked layers move in unison.

■ You can link as many layers as you like.

■ In this example, all the layers have been linked, including the Background layer.

BLEND LAYERS

You can use Elements' blending modes to specify how pixels in one layer blend with those in the layers below.

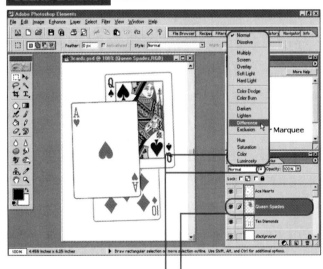

BLEND A REGULAR LAYER

1 Click the **Layers** tab to select the Layers palette.

Note: For more about opening and using palettes, see Chapter 1.

2 Click the layer that you want to blend.

3 Click 🔽 (🖨).

4 Click a blend mode.

■ Elements blends the selected layer with the layers below it.

■ This example shows the Difference mode, which creates a photo-negative effect where the selected layer overlaps other layers.

What effects do some of the different blending modes have?

The Multiply mode darkens the colors where the selected layer overlaps layers below it. The Screen mode is the opposite of Multiply; it lightens colors where layers overlap. Color takes the selected layer's colors and blends them with the details in the layers below it. Luminosity is the opposite of Color; it takes the selected layer's details and mixes them with the colors below it.

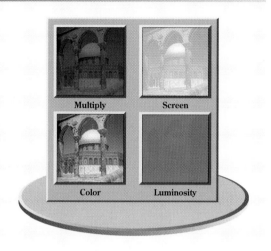

Multiply Screen

Color Luminosity

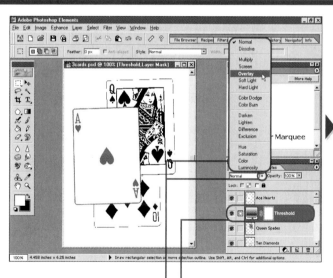 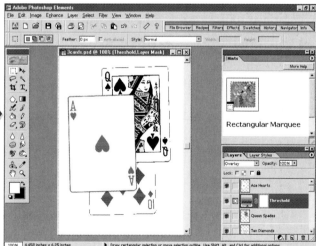

BLEND AN ADJUSTMENT LAYER

1 Click the **Layers** tab to select the Layers palette.

Note: For more about opening and using palettes, see Chapter 1.

2 Click an adjustment layer that you want to blend.

3 Click ▾ (⬍).

4 Click a blend mode.

■ Elements blends the selected layer with the layers below it.

■ This example shows the Overlay mode applied to a Threshold adjustment layer, which lets some of the original color through.

CHAPTER 9

Applying Effects and Styles

You can create special effects for your images by applying Elements' built-in effects. The effects let you add shadows, glows, and 3D appearances to your art. You can also add special effects to your layers with Elements' layer styles.

ADD A DROP SHADOW TO AN IMAGE

You can apply a drop shadow to make your image look like it is raised off the image canvas.

You can also apply a drop shadow to just a layer. See the section "Add a Drop Shadow to a Layer" for more information.

ADD A DROP SHADOW TO AN IMAGE

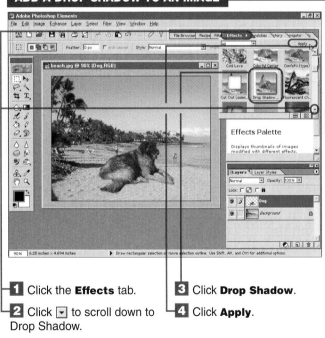

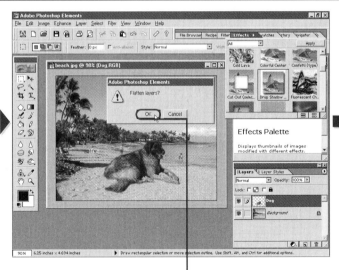

1 Click the **Effects** tab.

2 Click 🔽 to scroll down to Drop Shadow.

3 Click **Drop Shadow**.

4 Click **Apply**.

■ If you have a multilayered image, a dialog box appears asking if you want to flatten the layers.

5 Click **OK**.

Note: Because this effect flattens the layers in your image, it is best to apply it last.

What other shadow effects are there?

You can make a selection to your image and then apply the Cut Out effect. This erases the selected pixels and places a shadow along the edge of the cut-out.

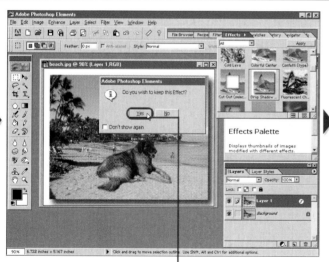

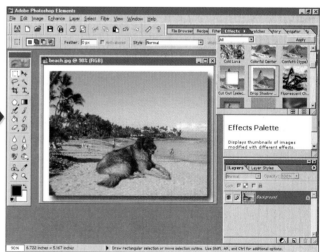

■ A dialog box appears asking if you want to keep the effect.

6 Click **Yes**.

■ You can click **No** to revert your image to its unchanged state.

■ Elements increases the canvas size and places an offset shadow under the image.

FRAME AN IMAGE

You can apply one of several frame styles to give your image a real-world look.

FRAME AN IMAGE

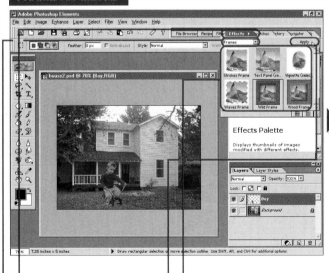

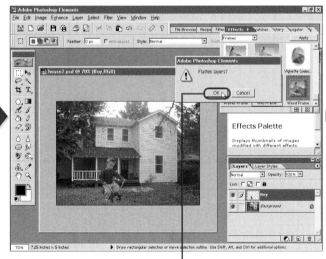

1 Click the **Effects** tab.

2 Click ▼ and click **Frames**.

3 Click an effect.

■ You can click ▼ to view other effects in the palette.

4 Click **Apply**.

■ If you have a multilayered image, a dialog box appears asking if you want to flatten the layers.

5 Click **OK**.

Note: Because this effect flattens the layers in your image, it is best to apply it last.

What are some of the types of frame effects in Elements?

You can give your art a modern look with a Brushed Aluminum Frame, create torn edges around your image with a Spatter Frame, or create a custom color border with a Foreground Color Frame. Click ▾ in the Effects palette to scroll through all the frame choices available.

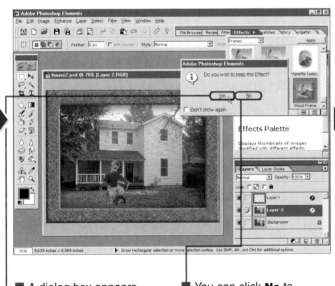

■ A dialog box appears asking if you want to keep the effect.

6 Click **Yes**.

■ You can click **No** to revert your image to its unchanged state.

■ Elements creates a frame around the outer edge of the image.

ADD A FANCY BACKGROUND

You add a fancy background to your image with one of Elements' several texture effects.

ADD A FANCY BACKGROUND

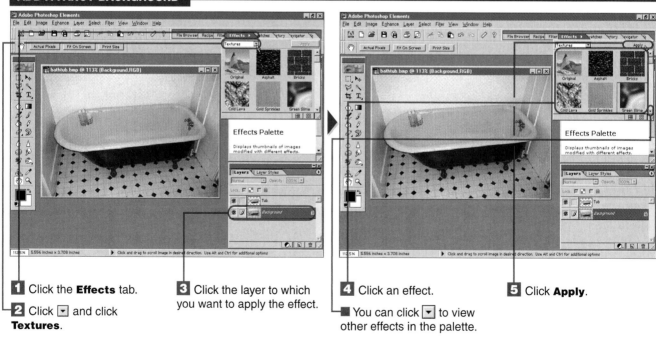

1 Click the **Effects** tab.

2 Click ▾ and click **Textures**.

3 Click the layer to which you want to apply the effect.

4 Click an effect.

■ You can click ▾ to view other effects in the palette.

5 Click **Apply**.

**How do I undo an effect after
I have applied it?**

Because Elements applies
effects in an automated
fashion using multiple
commands, you have
to click  multiple
times to undo an
effect. To see the
commands that were
involved, click the
History palette tab.

Soft Flat Color:
1. Duplicate Layer
2. Median
3. New Layer
4. Send Backward
5. Merge Down

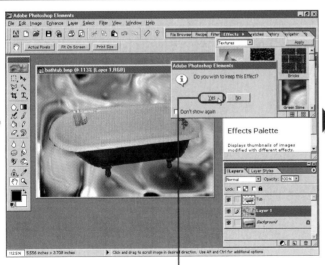

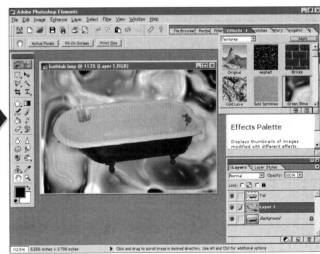

■ A dialog box appears
asking if you want to keep
the effect.

6 Click **Yes**.

■ You can click **No** to
revert your image to its
previous state.

■ Elements fills the layer
with the texture.

ADD A DROP SHADOW TO A LAYER

You can add a drop
shadow to a layer
to give objects a
3D look.

ADD A DROP SHADOW TO A LAYER

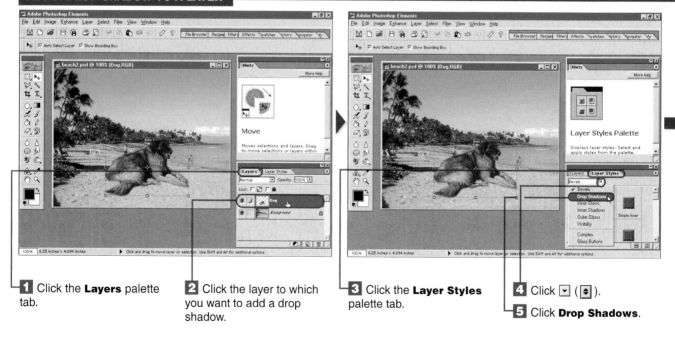

1 Click the **Layers** palette
tab.

2 Click the layer to which
you want to add a drop
shadow.

3 Click the **Layer Styles**
palette tab.

4 Click ⬛ (⬛).

5 Click **Drop Shadows**.

How do I add an inner shadow to a layer?

Click a layer and click **Layer**, **Layer Style**, and then **Inner Shadow**. An inner shadow causes the selected layer to appear to drop behind the image canvas.

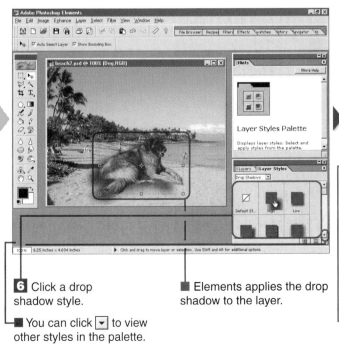

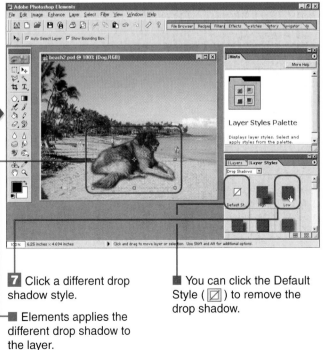

6 Click a drop shadow style.

■ You can click ▾ to view other styles in the palette.

■ Elements applies the drop shadow to the layer.

7 Click a different drop shadow style.

■ Elements applies the different drop shadow to the layer.

■ You can click the Default Style (▱) to remove the drop shadow.

ADD BEVELING TO A LAYER

You can bevel a layer to give it a three-dimensional look.

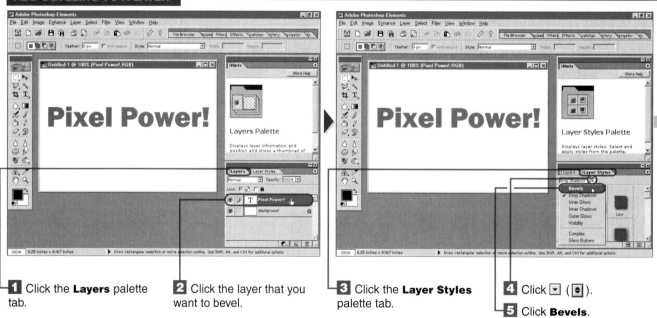

1 Click the **Layers** palette tab.

2 Click the layer that you want to bevel.

3 Click the **Layer Styles** palette tab.

4 Click ▼ (⬍).

5 Click **Bevels**.

When would I use the bevel style?

You may find this effect useful for creating three-dimensional buttons for Web pages. For example, to create such a 3D button, you can apply beveling to a colored rectangle and then lay type over it. See Chapter 6 for details about creating button shapes.

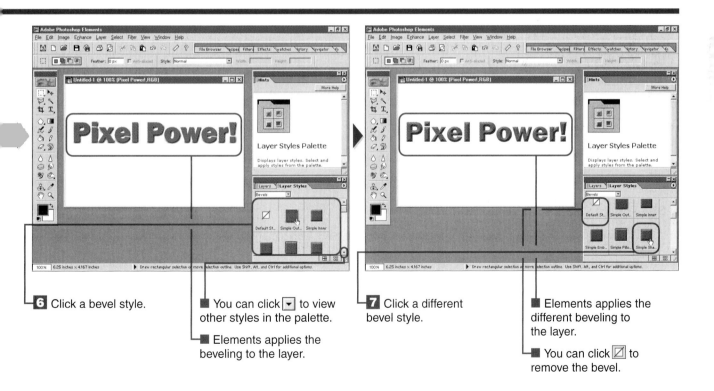

6 Click a bevel style.

■ You can click ▼ to view other styles in the palette.

■ Elements applies the beveling to the layer.

7 Click a different bevel style.

■ Elements applies the different beveling to the layer.

■ You can click ▨ to remove the bevel.

ADD AN OUTER GLOW TO A LAYER

The outer glow style adds faint coloring to the outside edge of a layer which can help highlight it.

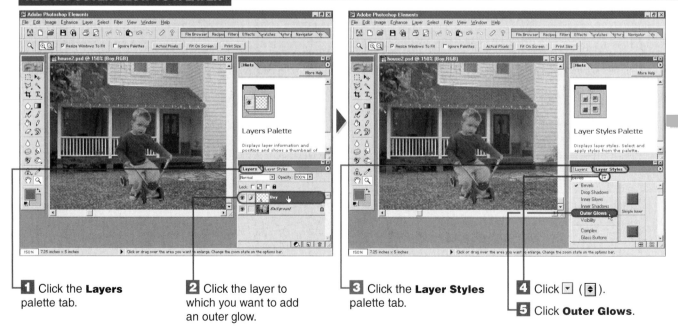

1 Click the **Layers** palette tab.

2 Click the layer to which you want to add an outer glow.

3 Click the **Layer Styles** palette tab.

4 Click 🔽 (🔽).

5 Click **Outer Glows**.

Can I add an inner glow to layer objects?

Yes, you can. Click ▼ in the Layer Styles palette and select **Inner Glows**. An inner glow adds color to the inside edge of a layer object.

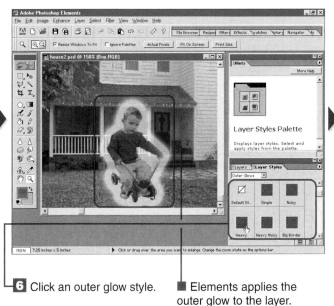

6 Click an outer glow style.

■ Elements applies the outer glow to the layer.

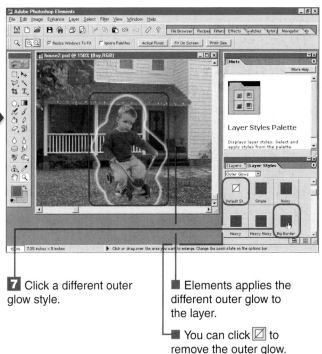

7 Click a different outer glow style.

■ Elements applies the different outer glow to the layer.

■ You can click ☐ to remove the outer glow.

EDIT A LAYER STYLE

You can edit a layer style that you have applied to your art. This lets you fine-tune the effect to achieve an appearance that suits you.

EDIT A LAYER STYLE

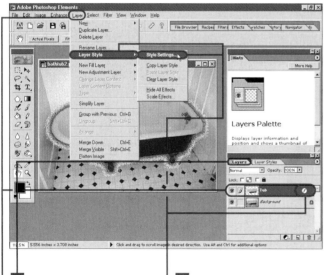

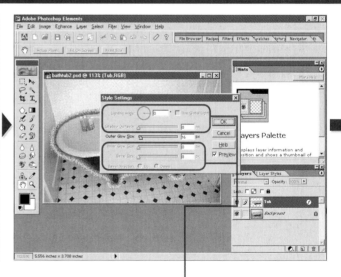

1 Click the **Layers** palette tab.

2 Click the layer whose style you want to edit.

3 Click **Layer**.

4 Click **Layer Style**.

5 Click **Style Settings**.

■ You can also double-click the ⓕ in the Layers palette.

■ Elements displays the current settings for the style.

■ Elements grays out settings for the styles that have not been applied.

Is there another way to change how styles affect my layers?

You can scale the intensity of applied styles by selecting the layer and clicking **Layer**, then **Layer Style**, and then **Scale Effects**. A dialog box appears allowing you to type a value to scale the effects from 1% to 1000%.

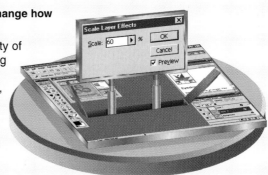

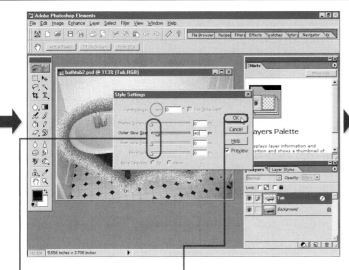

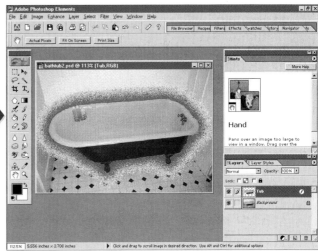

6 Click and drag the sliders to edit the values in the Style Settings dialog box.

■ This example shows an outer glow style increased in size.

7 Click **OK**.

■ Elements applies the edited style to the layer.

CHAPTER 10

Applying Filters

With Elements' filters, you can quickly and easily apply enhancements to your image, including artistic effects, texture effects, and distortions. Filters can help you correct defects in your images or let you turn a photograph into something resembling an impressionist painting. Elements comes with over 100 filters; this chapter highlights some of the more popular ones. For details about all the filters, see the Help documentation.

TURN AN IMAGE INTO A PAINTING

You can use many of Elements' artistic filters to make your image look as if you created it with a paintbrush. The Dry Brush filter, for example, applies a painted effect by converting similarly colored areas in your image to solid colors.

To apply the filter to just part of your image, select that part with a selection tool. See Chapter 4 to learn more about selection tools.

TURN AN IMAGE INTO A PAINTING

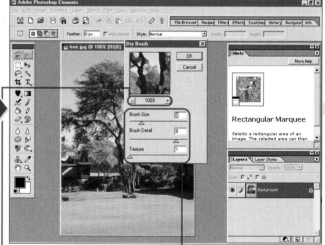

1 Select the layer to which you want to apply the filter.

Note: For more about layers, see Chapter 8.

■ In this example, the image has a single background layer.

2 Click **Filter**.

3 Click **Artistic**.

4 Click **Dry Brush**.

■ The Dry Brush dialog box appears.

■ A small window displays a preview of the filter's effect.

5 Click □ or □ to zoom out or in.

6 Fine-tune the filter effect by typing values for the Brush Size, Brush Detail, and Texture.

What does the Sponge filter do?

The Sponge filter reduces detail and modifies the shapes in an image to create the effect you get when applying a damp sponge to a wet painting. Apply it by clicking **Filter, Artistic,** and then **Sponge.**

■ This example shows how to thicken the dry-brush effect by increasing Brush Size and decreasing Brush Detail.

7 Click **OK**.

■ Elements applies the filter.

BLUR AN IMAGE

Elements' Blur filters reduce the amount of detail in your image. The Gaussian Blur filter has advantages over the other Blur filters in that you can control the amount of blur that you add.

To apply the filter to just part of your image, select that part with a selection tool. See Chapter 4 to learn more about selection tools.

BLUR AN IMAGE

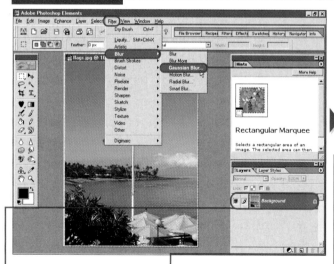

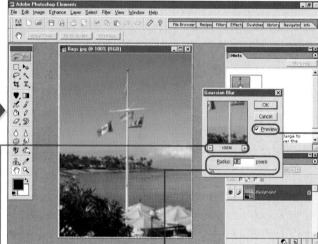

■1 Select the layer to which you want to apply the filter.

Note: For more about layers, see Chapter 8.

■ In this example, the image has a single background layer.

■2 Click **Filter**.

■3 Click **Blur**.

■4 Click **Gaussian Blur**.

■ The Gaussian Blur dialog box appears.

■ A small window displays a preview of the filter's effect.

■5 Click ⊟ or ⊞ to zoom out or in.

■6 Click **Preview** to preview the effect in the main window (☐ changes to ☑).

■7 Click and drag the Radius slider (△) to control the amount of blur.

How do I add directional blurring to an image?

You can add directional blur to your image with the Motion Blur filter. This can add a sense of motion to your image. Apply it by selecting **Filter, Blur,** and then **Motion Blur.**

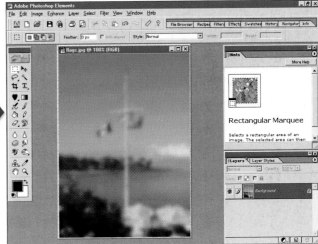

■ In this example, the amount of blur has been increased by boosting the Radius value.

8 Click **OK**.

■ Elements applies the filter.

SHARPEN AN IMAGE

Photoshop's Sharpen filters intensify the detail and reduce blurring in your image. The Unsharp Mask filter has advantages over the other Sharpen filters in that it lets you control the amount of sharpening you apply.

To apply the filter to just part of your image, select that part with a selection tool. See Chapter 4 to learn more about selection tools.

SHARPEN AN IMAGE

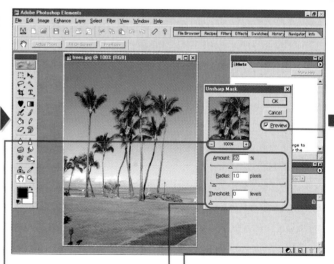

1 Select the layer to which you want to apply the filter.

Note: For more about layers, see Chapter 8.

■ In this example, the image has a single background layer.

2 Click **Filter**.

3 Click **Sharpen**.

4 Click **Unsharp Mask**.

■ The Unsharp Mask dialog box appears.

■ A small window displays a preview of the filter's effect.

5 Click ☐ or ✚ to zoom out or in.

6 Click **Preview** to preview the effect in the main window (☐ changes to ☑).

7 Click and drag the sliders (△) to control the amount of sharpening you apply to the image.

When should I apply sharpening?

Sharpening an image after you change its size is a good idea because changing an image's size adds blurring. Applying the Unsharp Mask filter can also help clarify scanned images.

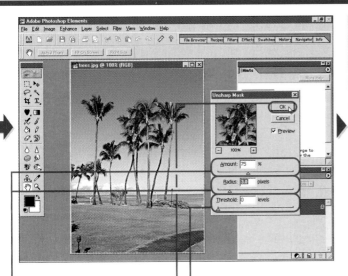

◼ **Amount** controls the overall amount of sharpening.

◼ **Radius** controls whether sharpening is confined to edges in the image (low Radius setting) or added across the entire image (high Radius setting).

◼ **Threshold** controls how much contrast you must have present for an edge to be recognized and sharpened.

8 Click **OK**.

◼ Elements applies the filter.

DISTORT AN IMAGE

Elements' Distort filters stretch and squeeze areas of your image. For example, the Spherize filter produces a fun-house effect. It makes your image look like it is being reflected off a mirrored sphere.

Another way to distort an image is by using the Distort command located under the Image menu. See Chapter 5 for more information.

To apply the filter to just part of your image, select that part with a selection tool. See Chapter 4 to learn more about selection tools.

DISTORT AN IMAGE

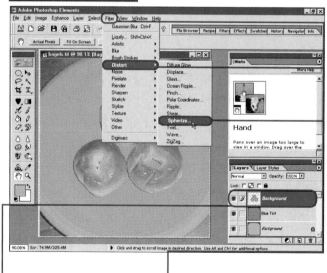

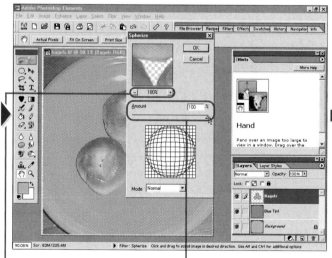

1 Select the layer to which you want to apply the filter.

Note: For more about layers, see Chapter 8.

2 Click **Filter**.

3 Click **Distort**.

4 Click **Spherize**.

■ The Spherize dialog box appears.

■ A small window displays a preview of the filter's effect.

5 Click ⬛ or ⊞ to zoom out or in.

6 Click and drag the Amount slider (◭) to control the amount of distortion added.

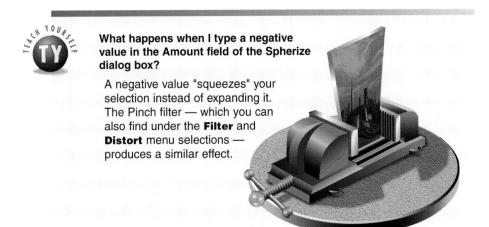

What happens when I type a negative value in the Amount field of the Spherize dialog box?

A negative value "squeezes" your selection instead of expanding it. The Pinch filter — which you can also find under the **Filter** and **Distort** menu selections — produces a similar effect.

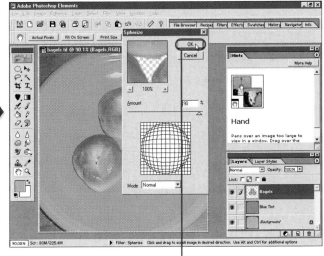

■ In this example, the intensity of the spherize effect has been decreased.

 Click **OK**.

■ Elements applies the filter.

ADD NOISE TO AN IMAGE

Filters in the Noise menu add or remove graininess in your image. You can add graininess with the Add Noise filter.

To apply the filter to just part of your image, select that part with a selection tool. See Chapter 4 to learn more about selection tools.

ADD NOISE TO AN IMAGE

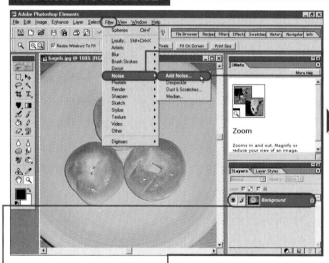

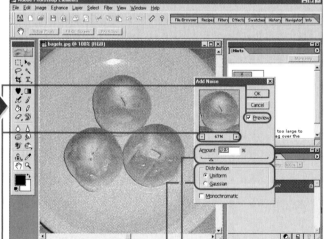

■1 Select the layer to which you want to apply the filter.

Note: For more about layers, see Chapter 8.

■ In this example, the image has a single background layer.

■2 Click **Filter**.

■3 Click **Noise**.

■4 Click **Add Noise**.

■ The Add Noise dialog box appears displaying a preview.

■5 Click □ or ⊞ to zoom out or in.

■6 Click **Preview** to preview the effect in the main window (☐ changes to ☑).

■7 Click and drag the Amount slider (△) to change the noise.

■8 Select the way you want the noise distributed (○ changes to ◉).

What does the Monochromatic setting in the Add Noise dialog box do?

If you click **Monochromatic** (☐ changes to ☑), Elements adds noise by lightening or darkening pixels in your image. Pixel hues stay the same. At high settings with the Monochromatic setting on, the filter produces a television-static effect.

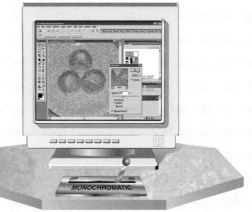

■ Uniform spreads the noise more evenly than Gaussian.

■ In this example, the Amount value has been decreased.

9 Click **OK**.

■ Elements applies the filter.

TURN AN IMAGE INTO SHAPES

The Pixelate filters divide areas of your image into solid-colored dots or shapes. The Crystallize filter, one example of a Pixelate filter, re-creates your image using colored polygons.

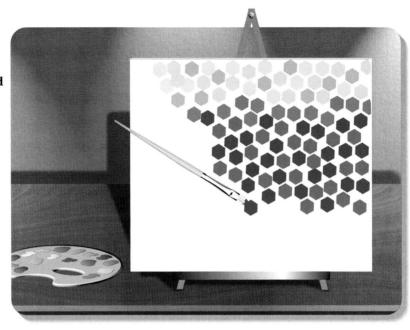

To apply the filter to just part of your image, select that part with a selection tool. See Chapter 4 to learn more about selection tools.

TURN AN IMAGE INTO SHAPES

1 Select the layer to which you want to apply the filter.

Note: For more about layers, see Chapter 8.

■ In this example, the image has a single background layer.

2 Click **Filter**.

3 Click **Pixelate**.

4 Click **Crystallize**.

■ The Crystallize dialog box appears.

■ A small window displays a preview of the filter's effect.

5 Click ⊟ or ⊞ to zoom out or in.

6 Click and drag the Cell Size slider (◺) to adjust the size of the shapes.

■ The size can range from 3 to 300.

What does the Mosaic filter do?

The Mosaic filter converts your image to a set of solid-colored squares. You can control the size of the squares in the filter's dialog box. Apply it by clicking **Filter, Pixelate,** and then **Mosaic.**

■ In this example, the Cell Size has been slightly increased.

7 Click **OK**.

■ Elements applies the filter.

TURN AN IMAGE INTO A CHARCOAL SKETCH

The Sketch filters add outlining effects to your image. The Charcoal filter, for example, makes an image look as if you have sketched it by using charcoal on paper.

The filter applies the foreground color as the charcoal color and the background color as the paper color. Changing these changes the filter's effect. See Chapter 7 to adjust color.

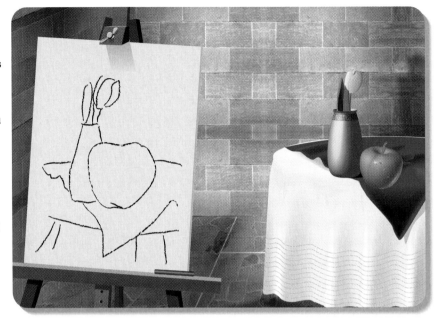

To apply the filter to just part of your image, select that part with a selection tool. See Chapter 4 to learn more about selection tools.

TURN AN IMAGE INTO A CHARCOAL SKETCH

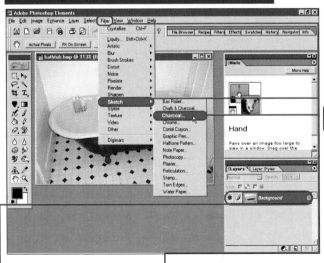

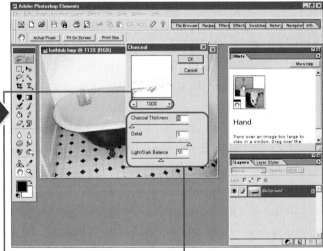

1 Select the layer to which you want to apply the filter.

Note: For more about layers, see Chapter 8.

2 Click **Filter**.

3 Click **Sketch**.

4 Click **Charcoal**.

■ The Charcoal dialog box appears.

■ A small window displays a preview of the filter's effect.

5 Click ⊟ or ⊞ to zoom out or in.

6 Click and drag the sliders (△) to control the filter's effect.

What does the Photocopy filter do?

The Photocopy filter converts shadows and midtones in your image to the foreground color and highlights in your image to the background color. The result is an image that looks photocopied. You can apply the Photocopy filter by clicking **Filter, Sketch,** and then **Photocopy.**

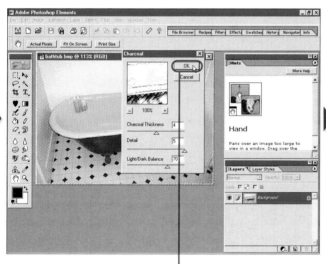

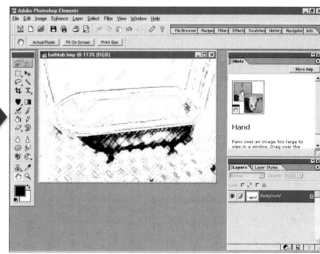

■ In this example, the thickness of the charcoal strokes has been increased. The Light/Dark Balance setting has also been increased to darken the image.

7 Click **OK**.

■ Elements applies the filter.

APPLY GLOWING EDGES TO AN IMAGE

The Glowing Edges filter, one example of a Stylize filter, applies a neon effect to the edges in your image. Areas between the edges turn black. Other Stylize filters produce similarly extreme artistic effects.

To apply the filter to just part of your image, select that part with a selection tool. See Chapter 4 to learn more about selection tools.

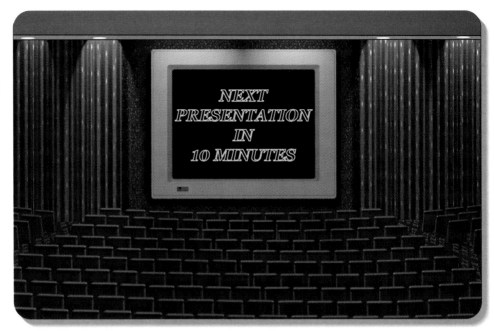

1 Select the layer to which you want to apply the filter.

Note: For more about layers, see Chapter 8.

■ In this example, the image has a single background layer.

2 Click **Filter**.

3 Click **Stylize**.

4 Click **Glowing Edges**.

■ The Glowing Edges dialog box appears.

■ A small window displays a preview of the filter's effect.

5 Click ☐ or ☐ to zoom out or in.

6 Click and drag the sliders (△) to control the intensity of the glow you add to the edges in the image.

How can I quickly add wild special effects to my images?

Many of the filters in the Stylize menu produce out-of-this-world effects. The Emboss and Solarize filters are two examples.

■ In this example, the Edge Width and Edge Brightness values have been increased to intensify the neon effect.

7 Click **OK**.

■ Elements applies the filter.

ADD TEXTURE TO AN IMAGE

You can overlay different textures on your image with the Texturizer filter. The other Texture filters let you apply other patterns.

To apply the filter to just part of your image, select that part with a selection tool. See Chapter 4 to learn more about selection tools.

ADD TEXTURE TO AN IMAGE

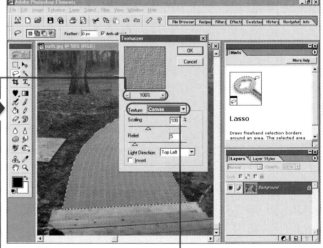

1 Select the layer to which you want to apply the filter.

Note: For more about layers, see Chapter 8.

■ In this example, the image has a single background layer.

2 Click **Filter**.

3 Click **Texture**.

4 Click **Texturizer**.

■ The Texturizer dialog box appears.

■ A small window displays a preview of the filter's effect.

5 Click ▭ or ⊞ to zoom out or in.

6 Click ▾ (⬍) and select a texture to apply.

What does the Stained Glass filter do?

The Stained Glass filter converts small areas of your image to different solid-colored shapes, similar to those you might see in a stained-glass window. A foreground-color border separates the shapes. Apply it by selecting **Filter, Texture,** and then **Stained Glass.**

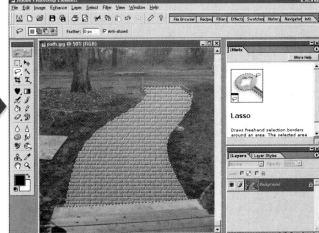

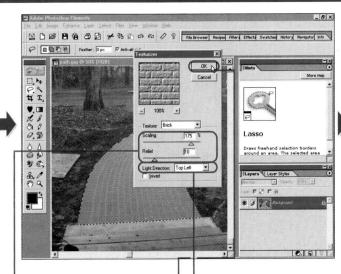

7 Click and drag the sliders (△) to control the intensity of the overlaid texture.

8 Click ☐ (☐) and select a Light Direction.

9 Click **OK**.

■ Elements applies the filter.

CAST A SPOTLIGHT ON AN IMAGE

The Lighting Effects filter lets you add spotlight and other lighting enhancements to your image. You may find it useful for creating ambiance in your photographic art.

To apply the filter to just part of your image, select that part with a selection tool. See Chapter 4 to learn more about selection tools.

CAST A SPOTLIGHT ON AN IMAGE

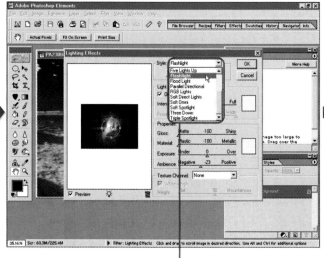

1 Select the layer to which you want to apply the filter.

Note: For more about layers, see Chapter 8.

■ In this example, the image has a single background layer.

2 Click **Filter**.

3 Click **Render**.

4 Click **Lighting Effects**.

■ The Lighting Effects dialog box appears.

■ Elements displays a small preview of the effect.

5 Click ▼ (▲) and click a lighting style.

What is a lens flare, and how can I add it to an image?

Lens flare is the extra flash of light that sometimes appears in a photo when too much light enters a camera lens. Photographers try to avoid this effect, but if you want to add it, you can use the Lens Flare filter. The effect can make your digital image look more like an old-fashioned photograph. Apply it by clicking **Filter, Render**, and then **Lens Flare.**

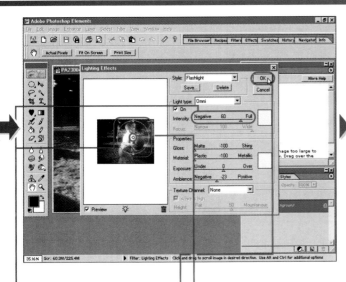

6 Click and drag the Intensity slider ( ) to control the light intensity.

7 Adjust the position and shape of the lighting by clicking and dragging the handles in the preview window.

■ You can click and drag the center point to change where the light is centered.

8 Click **OK**.

■ Elements applies the filter.

REMOVE DUST AND SCRATCHES

You can add slight blurring to your image to remove extraneous dust and scratches with the Dust & Scratches filter. This can help improve scans of old photographs.

REMOVE DUST AND SCRATCHES

1 Select the layer to which you want to apply the filter.

2 Select an area that has dust and scratches with a selection tool.

Note: For more about layers, see Chapter 8. To use the selection tools, see Chapter 4.

3 Click **Filter**.

4 Click **Noise**.

5 Click **Dust & Scratches**.

■ The Dust & Scratches dialog box appears.

■ Elements displays a small preview of the effect.

6 Click and drag the Radius slider (△) to control what size speck you consider dust or a scratch.

7 Click and drag the Threshold slider (△) to control how much the pixels need to differ from their surroundings for you to consider them a dust or a scratch.

What does the Dust & Scratches filter do to areas of an image that do not have dust or scratches?

Although the intention of the Dust & Scratches filter is to remove only minor artifacts from an image, it still adds some blur to wherever you apply it. For this reason, selecting areas that have dust and scratches before applying the filter is best. This prevents the filter from affecting details in an image unnecessarily.

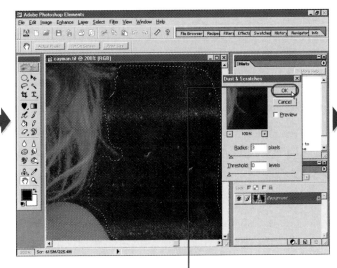

■ In this example, the Radius value has been increased slightly to remove all of the selected dust.

8 Click **OK**.

■ Elements applies the filter.

EMBOSS AN IMAGE

You can achieve the effect of a three-dimensional shape pressed into paper with the Emboss filter. This filter can be useful for generating textured backgrounds.

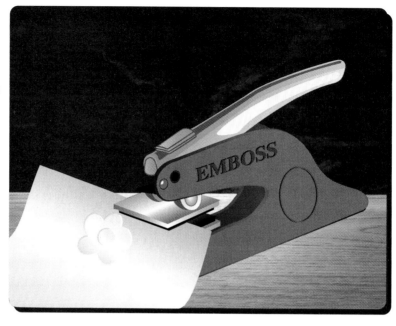

To apply the filter to just part of your image, select that part with a selection tool. See Chapter 4 to learn more about selection tools.

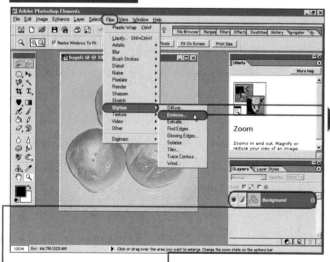

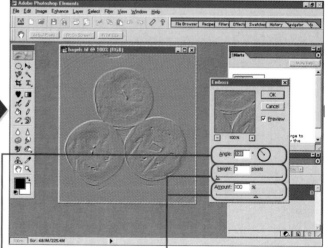

■1 Select the layer to which you want to apply the filter.

Note: For more about layers, see Chapter 8.

■ In this example, the image has a single background layer.

■2 Click **Filter**.

■3 Click **Stylize**.

■4 Click **Emboss**.

■ The Emboss dialog box appears.

■ Elements displays a small preview of the effect.

■5 Type an angle to specify in which direction to shadow the image.

■6 Type a height from 1 to 10 to specify the strength of the embossing.

■7 Type an amount from 1 to 500 to specify the number of edges the filter affects.

Do I have another way to create an embossed effect in an image?

You can use the Bas Relief filter to get a similar effect. Click **Filter, Sketch,** and then **Bas Relief.** It creates a two-toned embossed effect by reducing an image to the foreground and background colors.

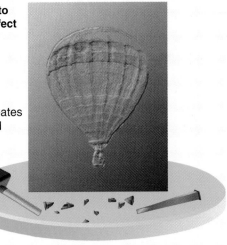

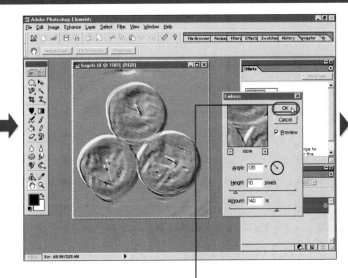

■ In this example, increasing the height and amount magnifies the Emboss effect.

8 Click **OK**.

■ Elements applies the filter.

CREATE A CUTOUT IMAGE

You can convert a detailed photograph into a relatively small number of solid-color blocks with the Cutout filter. The resulting image looks like it is made of construction-paper cutouts.

To apply the filter to just part of your image, select that part with a selection tool. See Chapter 4 to learn more about selection tools.

CREATE A CUTOUT IMAGE

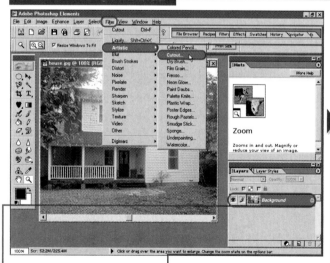

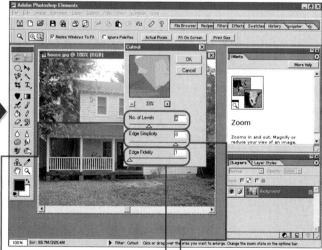

1 Select the layer to which you want to apply the filter.

Note: For more about layers, see Chapter 8.

■ In this example, the image has a single background layer.

2 Click **Filter**.

3 Click **Artistic**.

4 Click **Cutout**.

■ The Cutout dialog box appears.

■ Elements displays a small preview of the effect.

5 Drag the No. of Levels slider (△) to specify the number of colors in the resulting image.

6 Drag the Edge Simplicity slider (△) to specify the number of edges you find.

7 Drag the Edge Fidelity slider (△) to specify how well the solid-colored edges match the original edges.

How can I easily select the solid colors in an image that has the Cutout filter applied?

You can select the colors by using the Magic Wand tool with the tool's tolerance set to a low amount. For more information, see Chapter 4.

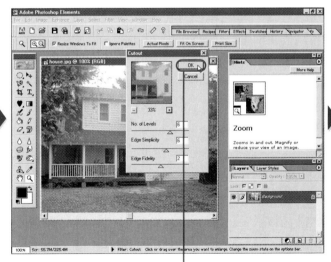

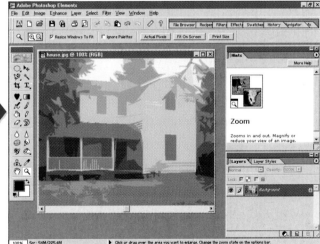

■ In this example, settings were adjusted to make the resulting image less abstract.

8 Click **OK**.

■ Elements applies the filter.

OFFSET AN IMAGE

The filters in the Other submenu produce interesting effects that do not fall under the other menu descriptions. For example, you can shift your image horizontally or vertically in the image window using the Other menu's Offset filter.

To apply the filter to just part of your image, select that part with a selection tool. See Chapter 4 to learn more about selection tools.

OFFSET AN IMAGE

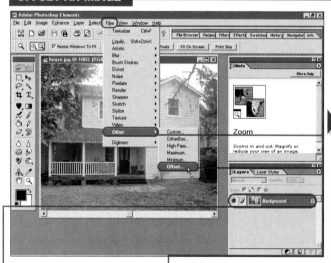

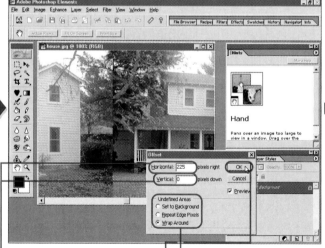

1 Select the layer to which you want to apply the filter.

Note: For more about layers, see Chapter 8.

■ In this example, the image has a single background layer.

2 Click **Filter**.

3 Click **Other**.

4 Click **Offset**.

■ The Offset dialog box appears.

5 Type a horizontal offset.

6 Type a vertical offset.

7 Select how you want Elements to treat pixels at the edge (○ changes to ◉).

8 Click **OK**.

How do I make a seamless tile?

Seamless tiles are images that when laid side by side leave no noticeable seam where they meet. You often use them as background images for Web pages. To create a seamless tile, start with an evenly textured image; then offset the image horizontally and vertically; then clean up the resulting seams with the Rubber Stamp tool ( ). See Chapter 6 for information on using the Rubber Stamp tool. The resulting image tiles seamlessly when you use it as a Web page background.

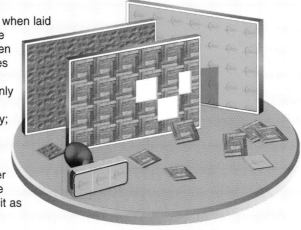

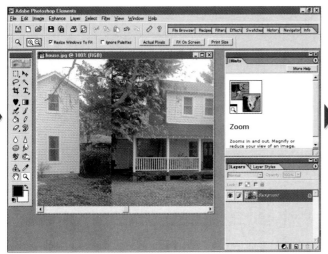

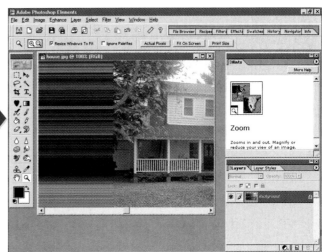

■ In this example, the image has been shifted horizontally (to the right) by adding a positive value to the horizontal field.

■ Wrap Around was selected, so the pixels that leave the right edge of the image reappear on the left edge.

■ In this example, the same offset was applied but with the Repeat Edge Pixels selected. This creates a streaked effect at the left edge.

USING THE LIQUIFY TOOLS

Elements' Liquify tools enable you to dramatically warp areas of your image. The tools are useful for making your image look like it is melting.

To apply the filter to just part of your image, select that part with a selection tool. See Chapter 4 to learn more about selection tools.

USING THE LIQUIFY TOOL

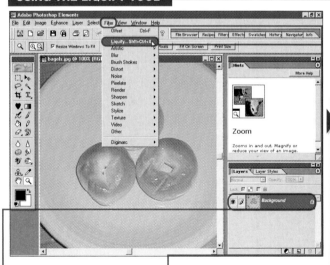

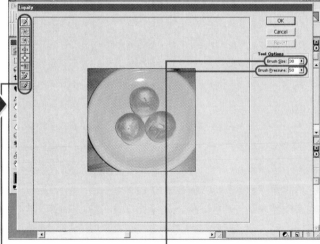

1 Select the layer to which you want to apply the Liquify tool.

Note: For more about layers, see Chapter 8.

■ In this example, the image has a single background layer.

2 Click **Filter**.

3 Click **Liquify**.

■ The Liquify dialog box displays.

4 Click a Liquify tool.

5 Type a Brush Size from 1 to 150.

6 Type a Brush Pressure (strength) from 1 to 100.

What do the different Liquify tools do?

The Warp tool () pushes pixels in the direction you drag.
The Twirl Clockwise tool ( ) twirls pixels clockwise.
The Twirl Counterclockwise tool ( ) twirls pixels counterclockwise.
The Pucker tool ( ) pushes pixels toward the brush center.
The Bloat tool ( ) pushes pixels away from the brush center.
The Shift Pixels tool ( ) pushes pixels perpendicular to the direction you drag.
The Reflection tool ( ) reflects pixels as you drag.
The Reconstruct tool ( ) restores pixels to their original state.

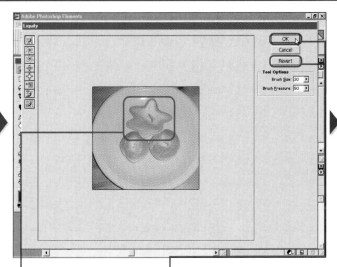

7 Click and drag inside the image window.

■ Elements liquifies the image where you drag the brush.

■ You can click **Revert** to change the image back to its original state.

8 Click **OK**.

■ Elements applies the Liquify effect to your image.

227

CHAPTER 11

Adding and Manipulating Type

Do you want to add letters and words to your photos and illustrations? Photoshop Elements lets you add type to your images and precisely control the type's appearance and layout. You can also stylize your type using Elements' filters and other tools.

ADD HORIZONTAL TYPE TO AN IMAGE

Adding type enables you to label elements in your image or use letters and words in artistic ways. You may find horizontal type useful for titles and captions.

ADD HORIZONTAL TYPE TO AN IMAGE

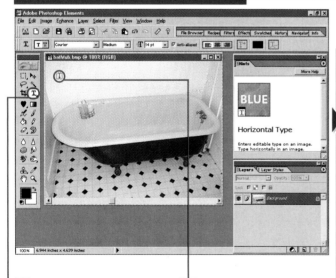

1 Click the Type tool (T).

2 Click where you want the new type to appear.

3 Click ▼ and select a font, style, and size for your type.

4 Click the color swatch to select a color for your type.

Note: Elements applies the foreground color by default. See Chapter 6 for more about selecting colors.

How do I reposition my type?

You can move the layer that contains the type with the Move tool (). Select the layer of type, click , and click and drag to reposition your type. For more on moving a layer, see Chapter 8.

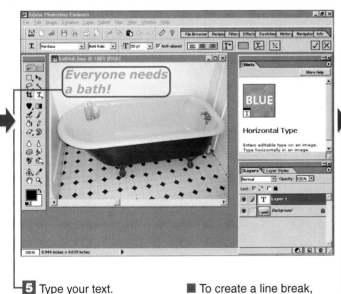

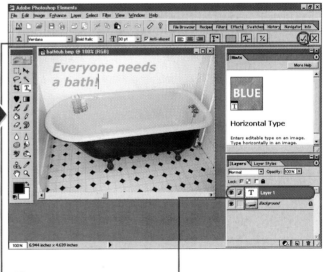

5 Type your text.

■ To create a line break, press Enter (Return).

6 After you finish typing your text, click ☑ or press Enter.

■ Elements places the type in its own layer.

ADD VERTICAL TYPE TO AN IMAGE

You can create vertical text to make interesting labels or signs in your images.

ADD VERTICAL TYPE TO AN IMAGE

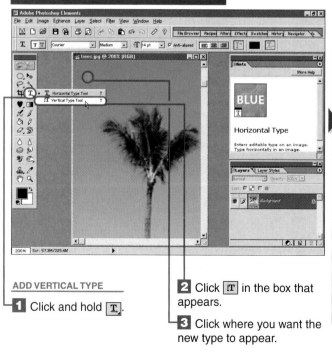

ADD VERTICAL TYPE

1 Click and hold 𝕋.

2 Click 𝕋 in the box that appears.

3 Click where you want the new type to appear.

4 Click ▾ and select a font, style, and size for your type.

5 Click the Color swatch (▢) to select a color for your type.

Note: Elements applies the foreground color by default. See Chapter 6 for more about selecting colors.

How do I change the alignment of my type?

When creating your text, click one of the three alignment buttons: Left align text (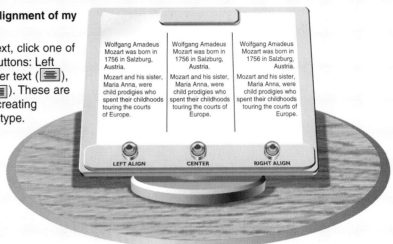), Center text (⎯), or Right align text (⎯). These are useful when you are creating multiline passages of type.

Wolfgang Amadeus Mozart was born in 1756 in Salzburg, Austria.

Mozart and his sister, Maria Anna, were child prodigies who spent their childhoods touring the courts of Europe.

Wolfgang Amadeus Mozart was born in 1756 in Salzburg, Austria.

Mozart and his sister, Maria Anna, were child prodigies who spent their childhoods touring the courts of Europe.

Wolfgang Amadeus Mozart was born in 1756 in Salzburg, Austria.

Mozart and his sister, Maria Anna, were child prodigies who spent their childhoods touring the courts of Europe.

LEFT ALIGN   **CENTER**   **RIGHT ALIGN**

6 Type your text.

■ The text appears vertically.

SWITCH THE TYPE TO HORIZONTAL

1 Click the layer containing the vertical type you want to switch.

2 Click the Change the Text Orientation button (T→).

■ Elements switches the vertical text to horizontal.

EDIT TYPE

You can edit type to change letters, words, or sentences.

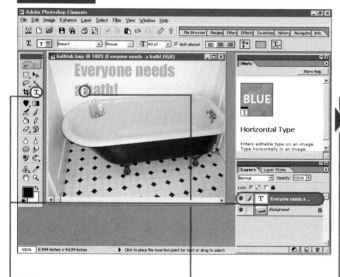

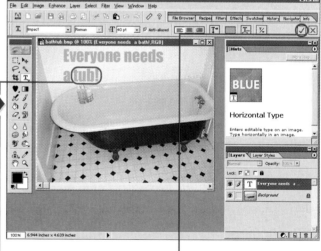

1 Click T.

2 Click the type layer that you want to edit.

*Note: If the Layers palette is not visible, you can click **Window** and then **Show Layers** to view it.*

3 Click inside the type at the place that you want to edit.

■ A blinking cursor (I) appears.

4 Press +Backspace or Delete to delete characters.

5 Type to add new characters.

6 After you finish typing your text, click ✓ or press Enter.

■ Elements applies your changes.

DELETE TYPE

You can delete a
type layer to remove
its type from your
image.

DELETE TYPE

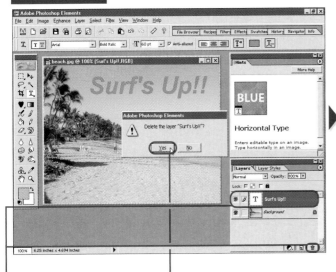

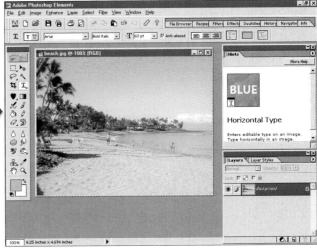

1 Click the type layer that
you want to delete.

2 Click 🗑.

■ A dialog box appears
asking if you want to delete
the layer.

3 Click **Yes**.

■ Elements deletes the layer
and the type inside it.

You can change the font, style, size, and other characteristics of your type.

CHANGE THE FORMATTING OF TYPE

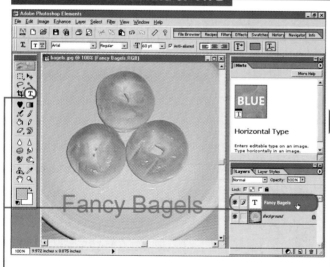

1 Click ![T].

2 Click the type layer that you want to edit.

*Note: If the Layers palette is not visible, you can click **Window** and then **Show Layers** to view it.*

3 Click and drag your cursor I to select some type from the selected layer.

■ You can double-click the layer thumbnail to select all the type.

How do I rotate type?

You can rotate type in your
image by rotating the layer
that contains the type.
Click the layer in the
Layers palette and
click **Image**, **Rotate**,
and **Free Rotate**. A
bounding box appears.
You can click and drag
outside the box to rotate the
layer. Click ✓ to apply the
rotation.

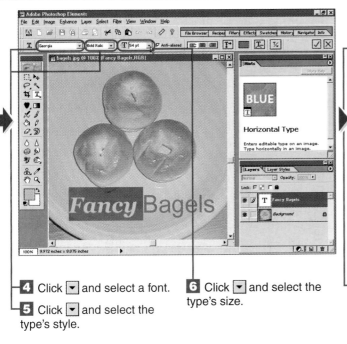

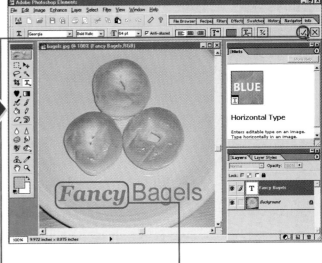

■ **4** Click ▼ and select a font.

■ **5** Click ▼ and select the type's style.

■ **6** Click ▼ and select the type's size.

■ **7** After you finish formatting your text, click ✓ or press Enter.

■ Elements applies the formatting to your type.

CHANGE THE COLOR OF TYPE

You can change the color
of your type to make it
blend or contrast with
the rest of the image.

CHANGE THE COLOR OF TYPE

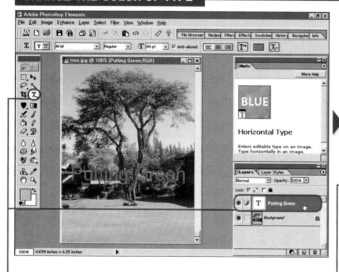

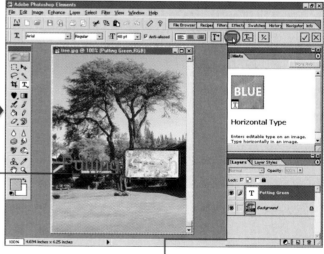

1 Click ⊤.

2 Click the type layer that
you want to edit.

*Note: If the Layers palette is not
visible, you can click **Window** and
then **Show Layers** to view it.*

3 Click and drag I to select
some text.

*Note: You can double-click the layer
thumbnail to select all the type.*

4 Click .

What is antialiasing?

Antialiasing is the process of adding semitransparent pixels to curved edges in digital images to make the edges appear more smooth. You can apply antialiasing to type to improve its appearance. Text that you do not antialias can sometimes look jagged. You can control the presence and style of your type's antialiasing with the Options bar.

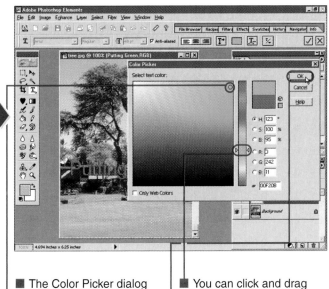

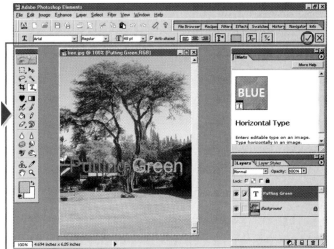

■ The Color Picker dialog box appears.

5 Click a color.

■ You can click and drag the slider (▷) to change the colors that Elements displays in the window.

6 Click **OK**.

7 Click ✓ or press `Enter`.

■ Elements changes the text to the new color.

APPLY A FILTER TO TYPE

You can add interesting effects to your type with Elements' filters. To apply a filter to type, you must first simplify it. Simplifying converts your type layer into a regular Elements layer. You can no longer edit simplified type using the type tools.

For more about filters, see Chapter 10.

APPLY A FILTER TO TYPE

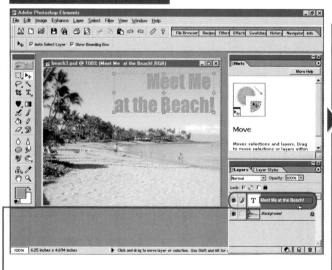

1 Select the type layer to which you want to apply a filter.

*Note: If the Layers palette is not visible, you can click **Window** and then **Show Layers** to view it.*

2 Click **Layer**.

3 Click **Simplify Layer**.

How can I create semitransparent type?

Select the type layer in the Layers palette and then reduce the layer's opacity to less than 100%. This makes the type semitransparent. For details about changing opacity, see Chapter 8.

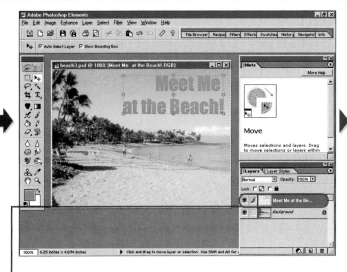

■ Elements converts the type layer to a regular layer.

■ Now you can apply a filter to the text.

■ In this example, a special effect was added to the type by clicking **Filter**, **Sketch**, and then **Bas Relief**.

WARP TYPE

Elements'
Warp feature
lets you easily
bend and
distort layers
of type.

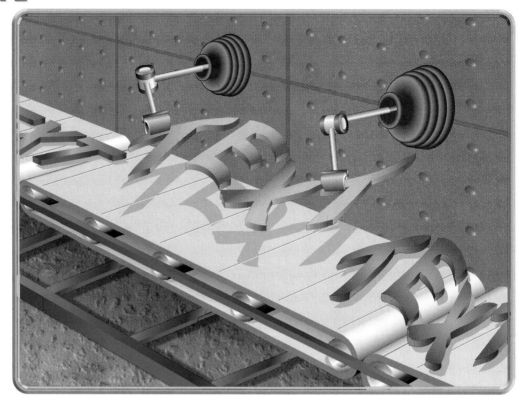

1 Click ![T].

2 Click the type layer that you want to warp.

*Note: If the Layers palette is not visible, you can click **Window** and then **Show Layers** to view it.*

3 Click the Create Warped Text button (![T..]).

■ The Warp Text dialog box appears.

4 Click the Style ▼ (🖢) and select a warp style.

How do I unwarp text?

Click the type layer that you want to warp and click the Create Warped Text button (🔲). Then click ▾ (🔲) and select **None** from the menu that appears. Click **OK** to unwarp the type.

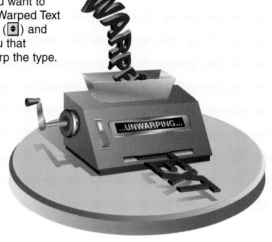

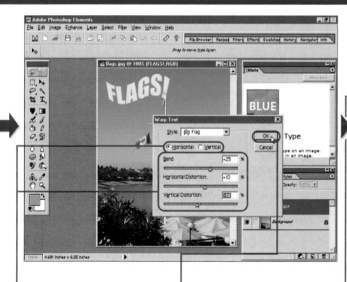

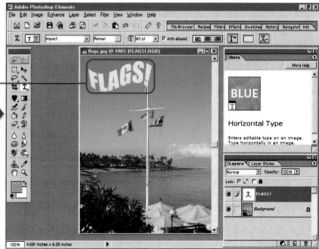

■5 Select an orientation for the warp effect (○ changes to ◉).

■6 Adjust the Bend and Distortion values by clicking and dragging the sliders (△).

■ The Bend and Distortion values determine how strongly Elements effects the warp. At 0% for all values, no warp is applied.

■7 Click **OK**.

■ Elements warps the text.

■ You can still edit the format, color, and other characteristics of the type after you apply warp.

OUTLINE TYPE

You can create
outlined type to give
letters and words in
your images a bold
look.

Outline Type is a type
of effect. For more
information about
Elements effects, see
Chapter 9.

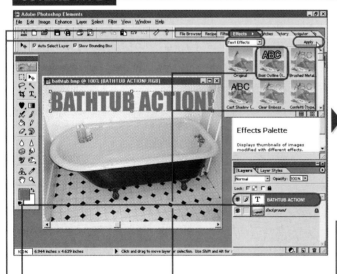

1 Click the type layer that
you want to outline.

2 Click the **Effects** tab.

3 Click ▾ (♦) and click
Text Effects.

4 Click an outline effect —
Thin Outline, Medium
Outline, or Bold Outline.

5 Click **Apply**.

■ A dialog box appears
asking if you want to keep
the effect.

6 Click **Yes** to keep the
effect.

■ You can click **No** to revert
your image to its unchanged
state.

You can cast a shadow next to your type to give the type a 3D look.

Cast Shadow is a type of effect. For more information about Elements effects, see Chapter 9.

CAST A SHADOW WITH TYPE

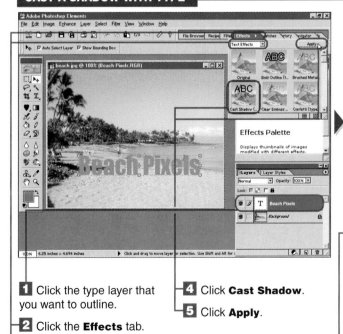

1 Click the type layer that you want to outline.

2 Click the **Effects** tab.

3 Click ▼ (🔁) and click **Text Effects**.

4 Click **Cast Shadow**.

5 Click **Apply**.

■ A dialog box appears asking if you want to keep the effect.

6 Click **Yes** to keep the effect.

■ You can click **No** to revert your image to its unchanged state.

CHAPTER 12

Automating Your Work

Sometimes you want to perform the same simple sequence of commands on a lot of different images. With Elements' batch commands, you can automatically convert the file type or change the size of every image file in a folder. Other Elements features make it easy to automatically create Web photo galleries, picture packages, and panoramic images.

CONVERT FILE TYPES

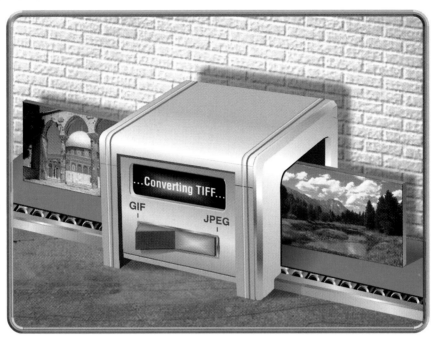

You can convert all the image files in a folder to a specific file type. You may find this useful if you want to post a number of pictures on the Web and need the images in a Web file format such as GIF or JPEG.

Before you can begin, you need to create a source folder and a destination folder for your images. To work with folders, see your operating system's documentation.

CONVERT FILE TYPES

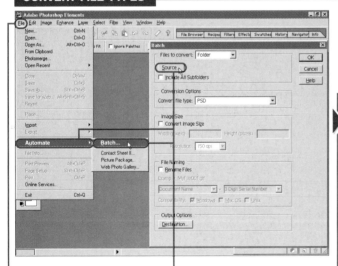

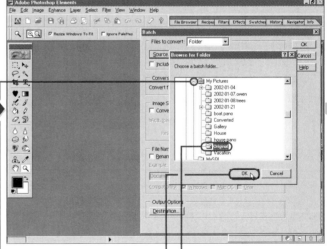

1 Place the images you want to convert into a source folder.

2 Create an empty destination folder in which to save your converted files.

3 In Elements, click **File**.

4 Click **Automate**.

5 Click **Batch**.

■ The Batch dialog box opens.

6 Click **Source**.

■ In Windows, the Browse for Folder dialog box appears. On a Mac, the Choose a batch folder dialog box appears.

7 Click ⊞ (▷) to open folders on your computer.

8 Click the folder containing your images.

9 Click **OK** (**Open**).

How do I rename the image files that I convert?

In the Batch dialog box, click **Rename Files** (☐ changes to ☑) and then click ▾ (◆) to select a naming scheme. Some of the options let you include a serial number or a date in the new file names. Elements displays an example of what the name of the converted file will look like in the dialog box.

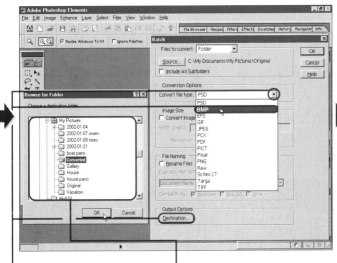

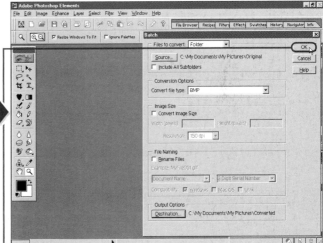

10 Click the Convert file type ▾ (◆).

11 Click a file type to which you want to convert.

12 Click **Destination**.

■ In Windows, the Browse for Folder dialog box opens. On a Mac, the Choose a destination folder dialog box appears.

13 Repeat steps **7** through **9** to select the folder where you want the converted files saved.

14 Click **OK**.

■ Elements converts the image files in the source folder and saves the new versions in the destination folder.

CONVERT IMAGE SIZES

You can resize all the image files in a folder to specific dimensions. You may find this useful if you want to quickly convert a number of large files from a digital camera to smaller versions that you can store and view more efficiently.

Before you can begin, you need to create a source folder and a destination folder for your images. To work with folders, see your operating system's documentation.

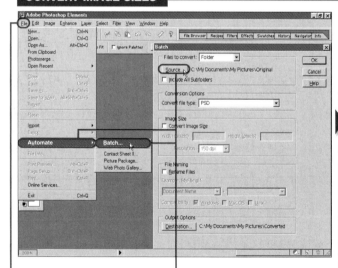

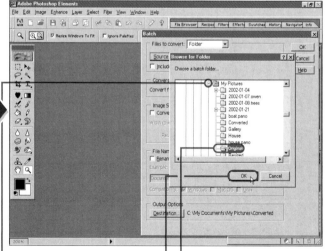

1 Place the images you would like to resize into a source folder.

2 Create an empty destination folder in which to save your resized files.

3 In Elements, click **File**.

4 Click **Automate**.

5 Click **Batch**.

■ The Batch dialog box opens.

6 Click **Source**.

■ In Windows, the Browse for Folder dialog box appears. On a Mac, the Choose a batch folder dialog box appears.

7 Click ⊞ (▶) to open folders on your computer.

8 Click the folder containing your images.

9 Click **OK (Open)**.

Can I batch process files that I currently have open in Elements?

Yes. Just select **Opened Files** from the **Files to convert** list in the Batch dialog box. Elements saves the processed files to the destination folder.

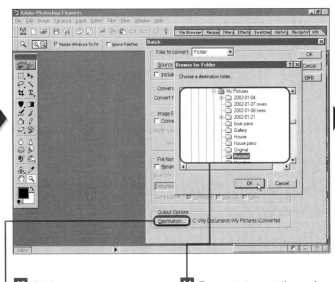

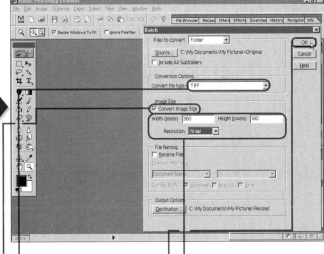

10 Click **Destination**.

■ In Windows, the Browse for Folder dialog box appears. On a Mac, the Choose a destination folder dialog box appears.

11 Repeat steps **7** through **9** to select the folder where you want the resized files saved.

12 Click the Convert file type ▼ (♦) and select a file type to save the resized files as.

13 Click **Convert Image Size** (☐ changes to ☑).

14 Type values for a new width, height, and resolution.

15 Click **OK**.

■ Elements resizes the image files and saves the new versions in the destination folder.

CREATE A CONTACT SHEET

Elements can automatically create a digital version of a photographer's contact sheet. Useful for keeping a hard-copy record of your digital images, contact sheets consist of miniature versions of images that often include identifying information.

For information about printing a contact sheet after you have created it, see Chapter 14.

CREATE A CONTACT SHEET

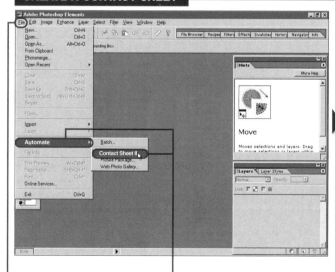

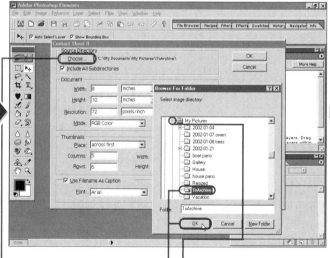

1 Place the images that you want on the contact sheet in a folder.

Note: To work with folders, see your operating system's documentation.

2 Click **File**.

3 Click **Automate**.

4 Click **Contact Sheet II**.

■ The Contact Sheet II dialog box opens.

5 Click **Choose**.

■ In Windows, the Browse For Folder dialog box opens. On a Mac, the Select Image Directory dialog box displays.

6 Click ⊞ (▶) to open folders on your computer (⊞ changes to ⊟).

7 Click the folder containing your images.

8 Click **OK**.

252

How do I make the thumbnail images larger on my contact sheet?

Paper size and the number of rows and columns automatically determine the size of the thumbnails. To change the thumbnail size, change the number of rows and columns you want on the sheet in the Columns and Rows boxes in the Contact Sheet dialog box.

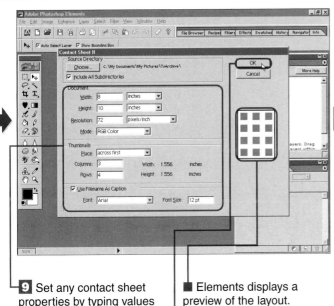

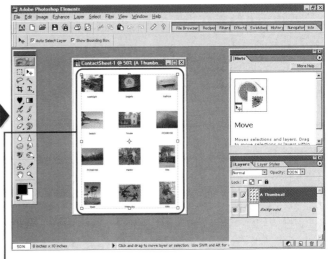

■9 Set any contact sheet properties by typing values or by clicking ▼ (♦) and selecting settings.

■ You can set contact sheet size and resolution, the order and number of columns and rows, and the caption font and font size.

■ Elements displays a preview of the layout.

■10 Click **OK**.

■ Elements creates and displays your contact sheet.

■ If there are more images than can fit on a single page, Elements creates multiple contact sheets.

CREATE A PICTURE PACKAGE

You can automatically create a one-page layout with a selected image at various sizes using the picture package command. You may find this useful when you want to print out pictures for friends, family, or associates.

For information about printing a picture package after you have created it, see Chapter 14.

CREATE A PICTURE PACKAGE

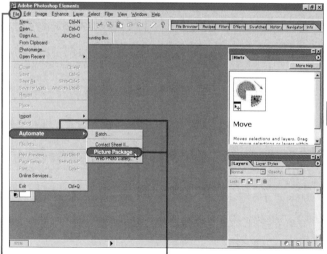

1 Click **File**.

2 Click **Automate**.

3 Click **Picture Package**.

■ The Picture Package dialog box displays.

4 Click **Choose**.

■ In Windows, the Select an Image File dialog box opens. On a Mac, the Please select a source file dialog box opens.

5 Click ▼ (◆) and select the folder that contains the image file.

6 Click the image file.

7 Click **Open**.

What size paper are the picture packages designed to print on?

If a package is prefixed with "11x17" in the Layout menu, it will fit on an 11-inch by 17-inch sheet of paper. All the other packages fit on an 8.5-inch by 11-inch sheet of paper.

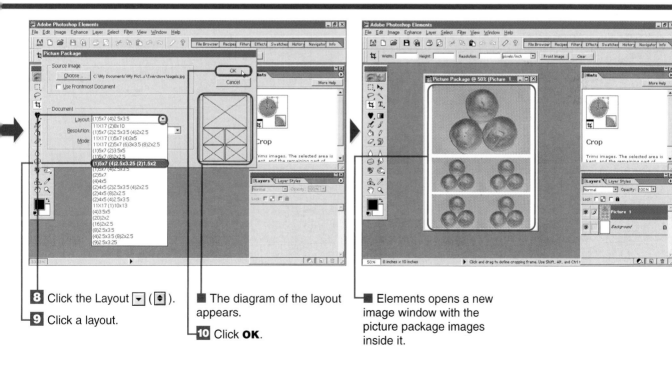

8 Click the Layout ▼ (🔽).

9 Click a layout.

■ The diagram of the layout appears.

10 Click **OK**.

■ Elements opens a new image window with the picture package images inside it.

CREATE A WEB PHOTO GALLERY

You can have Elements create a photo gallery Web site that showcases your images. Elements not only sizes and optimizes your image files for the site, but it also creates the Web pages that display the images and links those pages together.

After you create your photo gallery, you can use a Web publishing program such as Macromedia Dreamweaver or Adobe GoLive to upload your images to a Web server.

CREATE A WEB PHOTO GALLERY

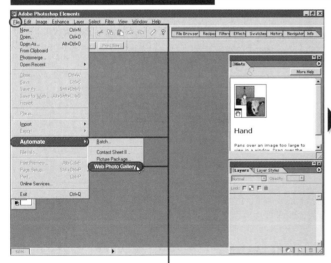

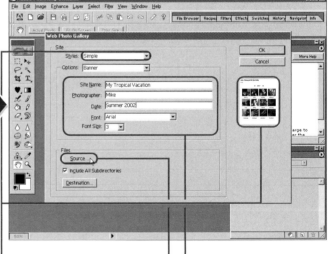

1 Place all the images you want to feature in your Web photo gallery in a folder.

2 Create a separate folder where Elements can save all the image files and HTML files necessary for your gallery.

Note: To work with folders, see your operating system's documentation.

3 Click **File**.

4 Click **Automate**.

5 Click **Web Photo Gallery**.

■ The Web Photo Gallery dialog box opens.

6 Click ▼ (♦) and select a photo gallery style.

■ Elements displays a preview of the style.

7 Type the title information for your Web pages.

8 Click **Source**.

How can I customize the pages in my Web photo galleries?

You can customize your pages by selecting different gallery styles in the Web Photo Gallery dialog box. The different styles organize the text and images in different ways on the Web pages. Some of the styles organize the gallery content into a framed Web site. You can also select different settings from the Options list to customize image sizes and colors for the gallery.

Vertical Frame Style

Table Style

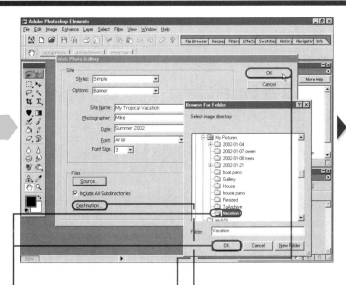

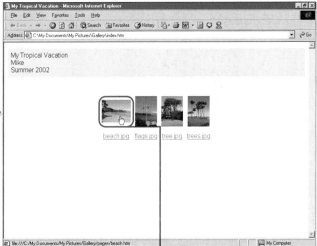

■ In Windows, the Browse for Folder dialog box opens. On a Mac, the Select image directory dialog box opens.

9 Select the folder containing your images.

10 Click **OK** (**Open**).

11 Click **Destination** and repeat steps **9** and **10** to specify the folder in which to save your gallery.

12 Click **OK** in the Web Photo Gallery dialog box.

■ Elements opens each image in the specified folder, creates versions for the photo gallery, and generates the necessary HTML code.

■ After the processing is complete, Elements opens the default Web browser on your computer and displays the home page of the gallery.

■ You can click a thumbnail to see a larger version of the image.

CREATE A PANORAMIC IMAGE

You can use the Photomerge feature in Elements to stitch several images together into a single panoramic image. A panoramic image allows you to display more scenery than is possible in a regular photograph.

Using a tripod to shoot pictures that will align correctly with the Photomerge feature is best.

CREATE A PANORAMIC IMAGE

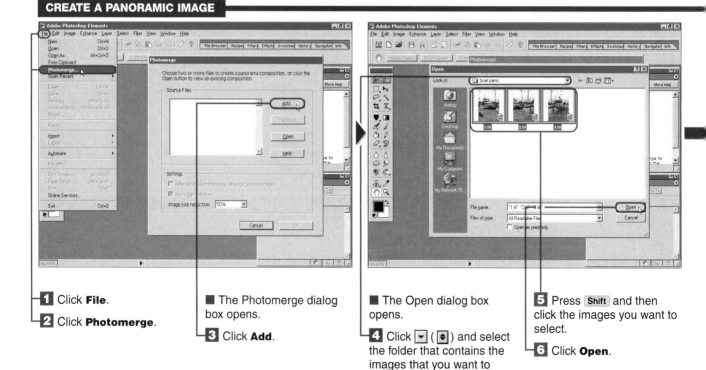

1 Click **File**.

2 Click **Photomerge**.

■ The Photomerge dialog box opens.

3 Click **Add**.

■ The Open dialog box opens.

4 Click ▼ (⬥) and select the folder that contains the images that you want to merge.

5 Press Shift and then click the images you want to select.

6 Click **Open**.

How can I create photos that will merge successfully?

To merge photos successfully, you need to align and overlap the photos. Here are a few hints:

- Use a tripod to keep your photos level with one another.

- Refrain from using lenses such as fisheye lenses that distort your photos.

- Shoot your photos so that they overlap at least 30%.

For more tips, see the Elements Help documentation.

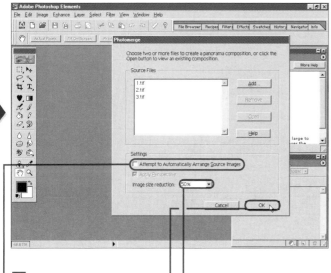

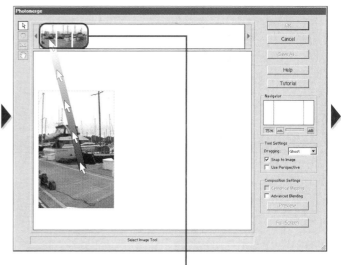

7 Deselect **Attempt to Automatically Arrange Source Images** (☑ changes to ☐).

■ You can optionally select an Image size reduction setting to shrink the source images before merging them.

8 Click **OK**.

■ Thumbnails of the selected images appear in a lightbox area.

9 Click and drag an image from the lightbox to the work area.

CONTINUED

CREATE A PANORAMIC IMAGE

The Photomerge dialog box allows you to interactively align the images that make up your panorama.

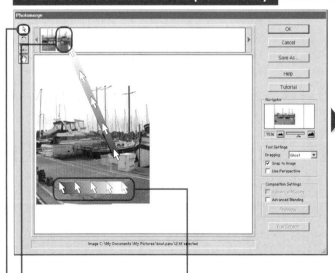

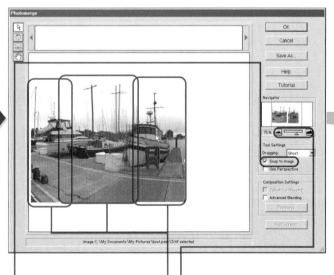

10 Click and drag another image from the lightbox to the work area.

11 Click the Select Image Tool ( ).

12 Click and drag the images so that they align with one another.

■ If you select **Snap to Image** (☐ changes to ☑), Elements tries to merge the image edges after you click and drag.

■ To fine-tune the adjustment, you can zoom in and out by adjusting the Navigator slider.

13 Repeat steps **10** through **12** for all of your images so that they overlap and match one another.

How do I apply perspective to my panorama?

You can select **Use Perspective,** and then use the **Vanishing Point Tool** () to specify the image that should serve as the central focal point for your panorama. When you apply this option, Elements warps the images next to the vanishing point image slightly to provide the correct perspective. The **Use Perspective** option is less useful for large panoramas — ones that cover more than 120 degrees.

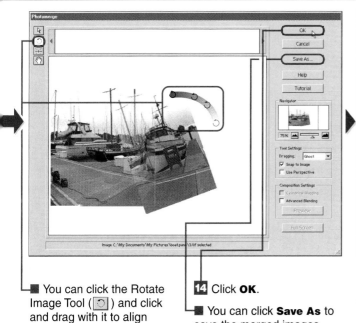

■ You can click the Rotate Image Tool (🔄) and click and drag with it to align image seams that are not level with one another.

14 Click **OK**.

■ You can click **Save As** to save the merged images directly to a file.

■ Elements merges the images and opens the new panorama in a new image window.

Note: To save the panorama, see Chapter 13. To print the panorama, see Chapter 14.

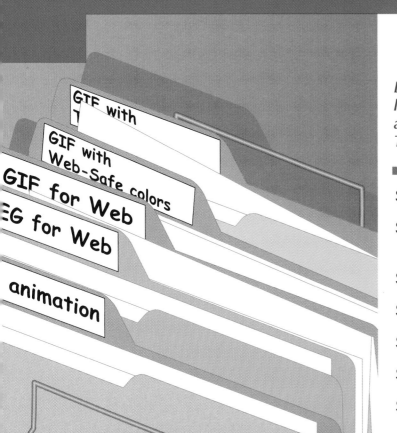

Saving Files

Do you want to save your files for use later? Or so that you can use them in another application or on the Web? This chapter shows you how.

SAVE IN THE PHOTOSHOP FORMAT

You can save your image in Photoshop's native image format. This format enables you to retain multiple layers in your image, if it has them. This is the best format in which to save your images if you still need to edit them.

SAVE IN THE PHOTOSHOP FORMAT

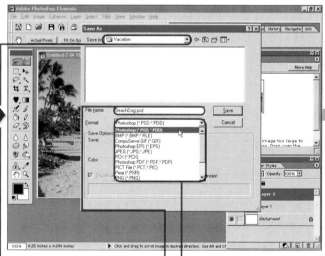

1 Click **File**.

2 Click **Save As**.

■ If you have named and saved your image previously and just want to save changes, you can click **File** and then **Save**.

■ The Save As dialog box appears.

3 Click ▼ (♦) and click a folder in which to save the image file.

4 Click ▼ (♦) and select the Photoshop file format.

5 Type a name for the image file.

■ Elements automatically assigns a `.psd` extension.

How do I choose a file format for my image?

You should choose the format based on how you want to use the image. If it is a multilayered image and you want to preserve the layers, save it as a Photoshop file. If you want to use it in word processing or page layout applications, save it as a TIFF or EPS file. If you want to use it on the Web, save it as a JPEG or GIF file. For more information on file formats, see the rest of this chapter as well as Elements' documentation.

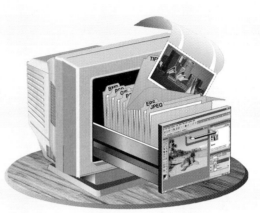

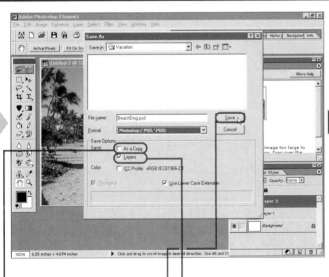

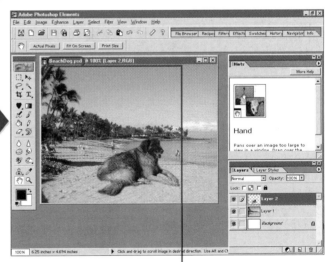

■ If you want to save a copy of the file and keep the existing file open, click **As a Copy** (☐ changes to ☑).

■ If you want to merge the multiple layers of your image into one layer, click **Layers** (☑ changes to ☐).

6 Click **Save**.

■ Elements saves the image file.

■ The name of the file displays in the image's title bar.

SAVE AN IMAGE FOR USE IN ANOTHER APPLICATION

You can save your image in a format that users can open and use in other imaging or page-layout applications. TIFF, or Tagged Image File Format, and EPS, or Encapsulated PostScript, are standard printing formats that many applications on both Windows and Macintosh platforms support.

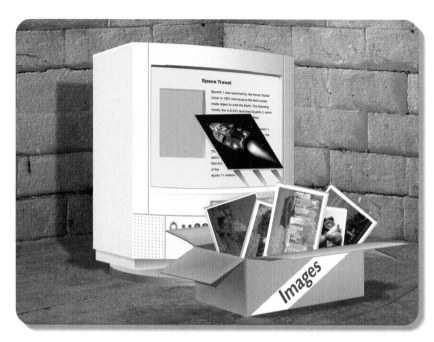

Most image formats — with the exception of the Photoshop format — do not support layers.

SAVE AN IMAGE FOR USE IN ANOTHER APPLICATION

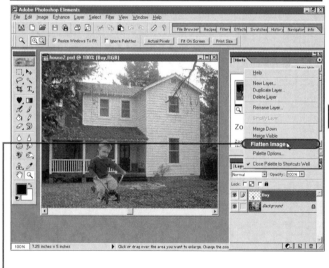

1 Click the Layers and click **Flatten Image**.

■ If you do not have multiple layers, skip to step **2**.

■ The layers combine into a single layer.

2 Click **File**.

3 Click **Save As**.

■ The Save As dialog box appears.

What are some popular page-layout programs with which I might use images?

Adobe InDesign and QuarkXPress are two popular page-layout programs. They let you combine text and images to create brochures, magazines, and other printed media. You can import TIFF and EPS files saved in Elements into both programs.

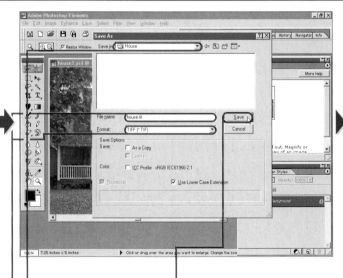

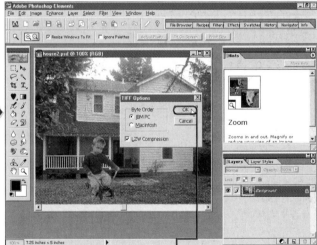

4 Click ▼ (●) and choose a folder in which to save the image file.

5 Click ▼ (●) and select a file format.

6 Type a filename.

■ Elements automatically assigns an appropriate extension for the file format, such as .tif for TIFF or .eps for EPS.

7 Click **Save**.

■ In this example, the TIFF format was selected.

■ A dialog box appears, enabling you to specify the type of TIFF you want to save.

8 Click **OK**.

■ Elements saves your image.

SAVE A JPEG FOR THE WEB

You can save a file in the JPEG — Joint Photographic Experts Group — format and publish it on the Web. JPEG is the preferred file format for saving photographic images.

SAVE A JPEG FOR THE WEB

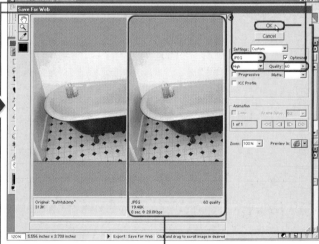

1 Click **File**.

2 Click **Save for Web**.

■ The Save For Web dialog box appears.

3 Click ▼ (♦) and select **JPEG**.

4 Select a JPEG quality setting.

■ You can select a descriptive setting or a numeric value from 0, low quality, to 100, high quality.

■ The higher the quality, the larger the resulting file.

5 Check that the file quality and size are acceptable in the preview window.

6 Click **OK**.

What is image compression?

Image compression involves using mathematical techniques to reduce the amount of information required to describe an image. This results in small file sizes, which is important when transmitting information on the Web. Some compression schemes, such as JPEG, involve some loss in quality due to the compression, but the loss is usually negligible compared to the file size savings.

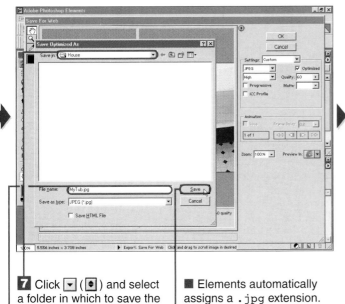

7 Click (▼) and select a folder in which to save the file.

8 Type a filename.

■ Elements automatically assigns a `.jpg` extension.

9 Click **Save**.

■ Elements saves the JPEG file in the specified folder.

■ You can open the folder to access the file.

■ The original image file remains open in Elements.

SAVE A GIF FOR THE WEB

You can save a file as a GIF — Graphics Interchange Format — and publish it on the Web. The GIF format is good for saving illustrations that have a lot of solid color. The format supports a maximum of 256 colors.

SAVE A GIF FOR THE WEB

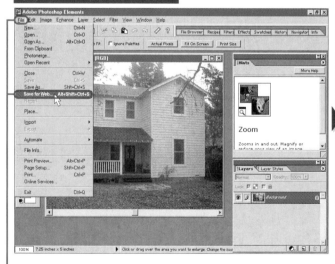

1 Click **File**.

2 Click **Save for Web**.

■ The Save For Web dialog box appears.

3 Click ▼ (🔁) and select **GIF**.

4 Click 🔁 and select the number of colors to include in the image.

■ GIF allows a maximum of 256 colors, making it unsuitable for many photos.

5 Check that the file quality and size are acceptable in the preview window.

6 Click **OK**.

How do I minimize the file sizes of my GIF images?

The most important factor in creating small GIFs is limiting the number of colors in the final image. GIF files are limited to 256 colors or fewer. In images that have just a few solid colors, you can often reduce the total number of colors to 16 or 8 without any noticeable reduction in quality. See step **4** below for setting the number of colors in your GIF images.

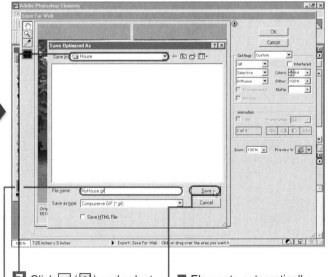

7 Click ▼ (🔽) and select a folder in which to save the file.

8 Type a filename.

■ Elements automatically assigns a `.gif` extension.

9 Click **Save**.

■ Elements saves the GIF file in the specified folder.

■ You can open the folder to access the file.

■ The original image file remains open in Elements.

SAVE A GIF WITH TRANSPARENCY

You can include transparency in files saved in the GIF file format. The transparent pixels do not show up on Web pages.

Because Elements background layers cannot contain transparent pixels, you need to work with non-background layers to create transparent GIFs. See Chapter 8 for more about layers. The other Web file format, JPEG, does not support transparency.

SAVE A GIF WITH TRANSPARENCY

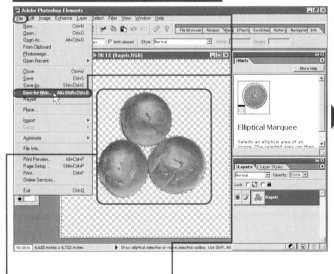

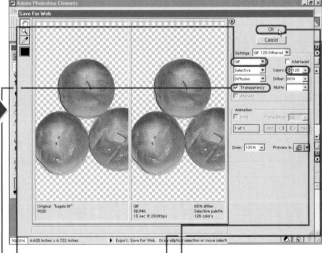

1 Select the area that you want to make transparent with a selection tool.

Note: See Chapter 4 to learn how to use the selection tools.

2 Press **Delete** to delete the pixels.

■ Elements replaces the deleted pixels with a checkerboard pattern.

3 Click **File**.

4 Click **Save for Web**.

5 Click ▾ (⬍) and select **GIF**.

6 Click **Transparency** to retain transparency in the saved file (☐ changes to ☑).

7 Click ⬍ and select the number of colors to include in the image.

■ GIF allows a maximum of 256 colors.

8 Click **OK**.

What file size should I make my Web images?

If a large portion of your audience uses 56K modems to view your Web pages, keep your images small enough so that total page size — which includes all the images on the page plus the HTML file — is below 50K. You can check the file size and the download speed of an image at the bottom of the Save For Web preview pane. To change an image's file size and download speed, you can adjust the quality and color settings in the Save For Web dialog box. See "Save a JPEG for the Web" and "Save a GIF for the Web" for details.

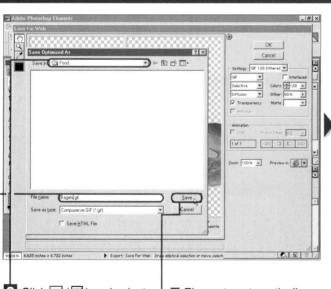

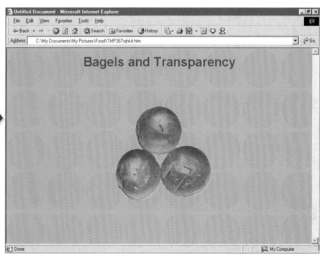

9 Click ▼ (🖢) and select a folder in which to save the file.

10 Type a name for the file.

■ Elements automatically assigns a .gif extension.

11 Click **Save**.

■ In this example, the image has been added to a Web page and opened in a Web browser.

■ The transparency causes the Web page background to show through around the edges of the image.

SAVE A GIF WITH WEB-SAFE COLORS

You can save your GIF images using only Web-safe colors. This ensures that the images appear the way you expect in browsers running on 256-color monitors.

You can create Web-safe images only in the GIF format.

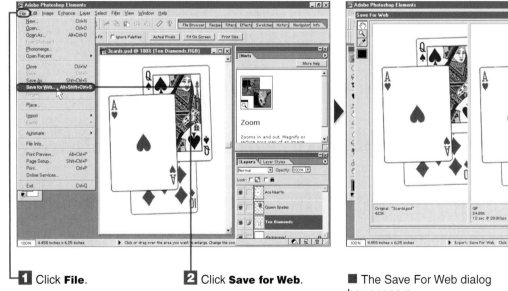

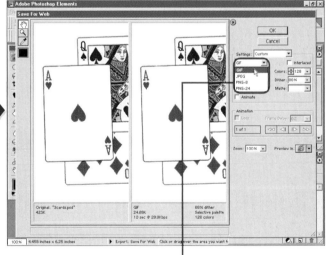

1 Click **File**.

2 Click **Save for Web**.

■ The Save For Web dialog box appears.

3 Click ▼ (⬍) and select **GIF**.

Should I save all my Web images with Web-safe colors?

Not necessarily. Nowadays, most people surf the Web on monitors set to thousands of colors or more, which makes Web safety less relevant. Also, it is better to save photographic Web images as non-Web-safe JPEGs because the GIF file format offers poor compression and quality when it comes to photos.

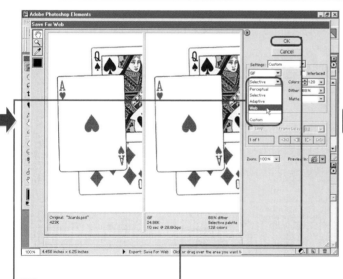

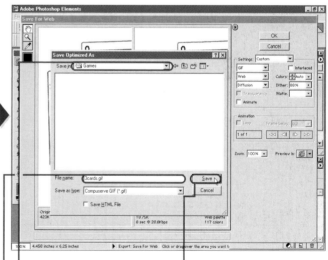

■ Click ▼ (◆) and select **Web** as the color palette type.

Note: When you do not specify Web-safe colors, Elements saves the image by choosing from all the colors available in the spectrum.

■ Elements now uses only colors from the palette available to browsers running on 256-color monitors.

■ Click **OK**.

■ Click ▼ (◆) and select a folder in which to save the file.

■ Type a name for the file.

■ Elements automatically assigns a .gif extension.

■ Click **Save**.

■ Elements saves the GIF file in the specified folder.

■ You can open the folder to access the file.

SAVE A GIF ANIMATION

You can create a multilayer Elements image and save it as an animated GIF file. Each layer serves as a frame in the animation. Frames are snapshots that show the animated object in different positions — like pages in a flip book.

Layer 1   Layer 2   Layer 3   Layer 4

You can view the animation in a Web browser.

SAVE A GIF ANIMATION

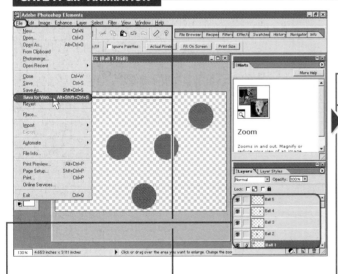

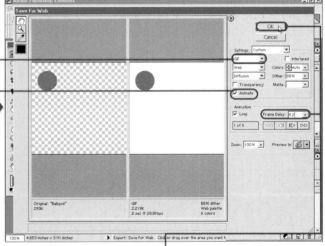

CREATE AN ANIMATION

1 Create a series of frames, placing each frame in a layer.

■ Each layer should display the animated object in a different position.

Note: For more about layers, see Chapter 8.

■ The first animation frame is the bottom-most layer.

2 Click **File**.

3 Click **Save for Web**.

■ The Save For Web dialog box appears.

4 Click ▼ (◆) and select **GIF**.

5 Click **Animate** (☐ changes to ☑).

■ You can click **Loop** to make the animation repeat.

6 Click ▼ (◆) and select a frame delay.

7 Click **OK**.

How do I create GIF animations that display effectively?

- Because GIF images only display 256 colors, create them with flat-color art rather than photographs.

- Because frame speeds vary across systems, test your animations on a variety of platforms and browsers.

- Because multiple animation frames quickly create a large file size, check the file size in the Save For Web preview pane.

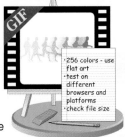

256 colors - use
flat art
test on
different
browsers and
platforms
check file size

How do I use the animation controls to test my animated GIF?

You can use the control buttons in the Save For Web dialog box to move between animation frames:

	Select First Frame .... Displays the first frame in your animation.
	Select Previous Frame .. Displays the previous frame in your animation.
	Select Next Frame .... Displays the next frame in your animation.
	Select Last Frame .... Displays the final frame in your animation.

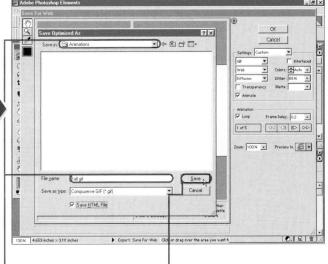

■ The Save Optimized As dialog box appears.

8 Click ▼ (◆) and select a folder in which to save the file.

9 Type a name for the file.

■ Elements automatically assigns a .gif extension.

10 Click **Save**.

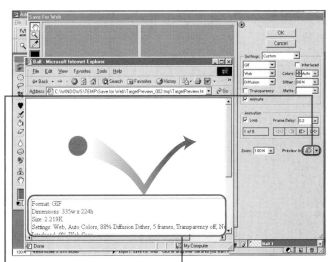

PREVIEW THE ANIMATION

1 Repeat steps **1** through **6**.

2 In the Save for Web dialog box, click 🖾.

■ The GIF animation opens in the browser and plays.

■ General information about the image file displays below the image.

ADD CAPTION AND COPYRIGHT INFORMATION

You can store caption and copyright information with your saved image. You may find this useful if you plan on publishing the images online.

Some image editing applications — such as Elements — can detect copyright information from an image and display it to a user who opens it.

Butterfly   Copyright © John Wiley

ADD CAPTION AND COPYRIGHT INFORMATION

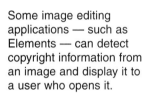

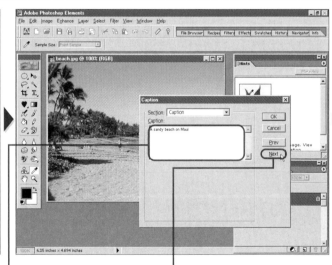

ADD A CAPTION

1 Click **File**.

2 Click **File Info**.

■ The Caption dialog box appears.

3 Type a caption for your image.

■ You can print the caption along with the image by selecting **Caption** in the Page Setup dialog box (☐ changes to ☑).

Note: See Chapter 14 for more on printing captions.

4 Click **Next**.

How do I retrieve information about a photo taken with a digital camera?

Information about photos taken with a digital camera is stored as EXIF information. You can view it in the Caption dialog box by clicking the Section ▼ (⬍) and selecting **EXIF**. This information includes the make and model of the camera and the date and time the photo was shot.

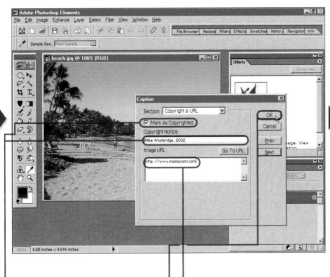

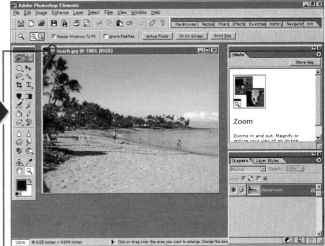

ADD COPYRIGHT INFORMATION

5 Click **Mark As Copyrighted** (☐ changes to ☑) to display a copyright symbol in the image window title bar.

6 Type a copyright notice.

■ You can type a Web address that you want to associate with the image.

7 Click **OK**.

■ Elements places a copyright symbol in the title bar.

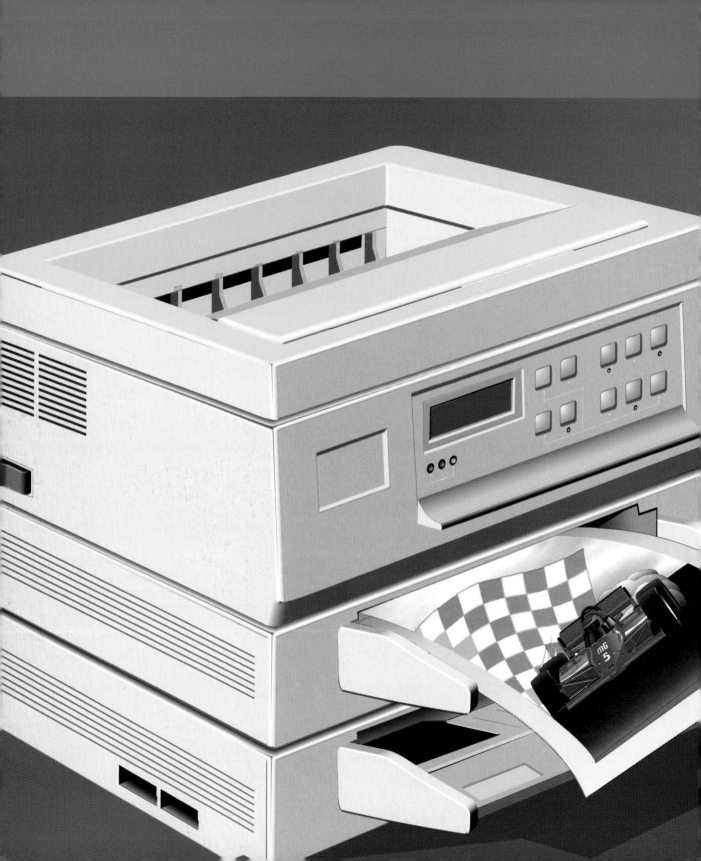

CHAPTER 14

Printing Images

Printing enables you to save the digital imagery you create in Photoshop Elements in hard-copy form. Elements can print to black-and-white or color printers.

PRINT AN IMAGE FROM A PC

You can print your
Photoshop Elements
image from a PC to
create a hard copy of
your work.

PRINT AN IMAGE FROM A PC

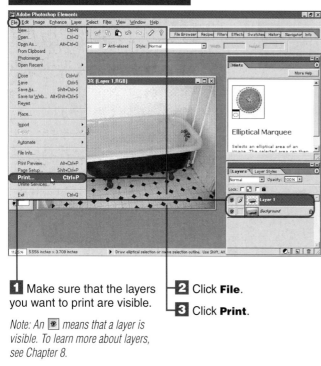

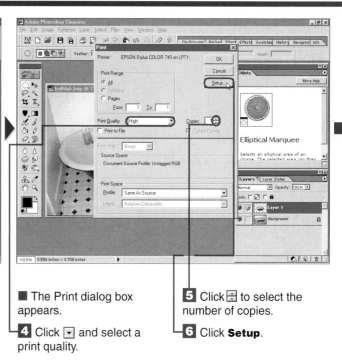

1 Make sure that the layers
you want to print are visible.

*Note: An ▣ means that a layer is
visible. To learn more about layers,
see Chapter 8.*

2 Click **File**.

3 Click **Print**.

■ The Print dialog box
appears.

4 Click ⯆ and select a
print quality.

5 Click ▦ to select the
number of copies.

6 Click **Setup**.

How do I include a description on my printout?

Click **Caption** (☐ changes to ☑) in the Page Setup dialog box to include a caption with your image. For details about specifying caption information, see Chapter 13.

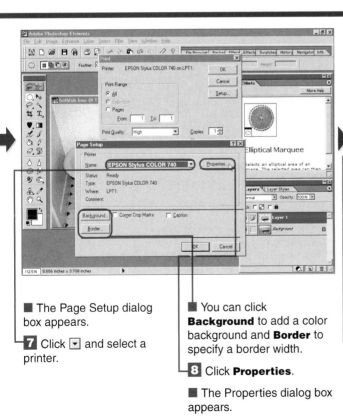

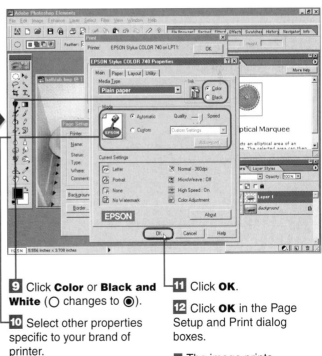

■ The Page Setup dialog box appears.

7 Click ▼ and select a printer.

■ You can click **Background** to add a color background and **Border** to specify a border width.

8 Click **Properties**.

■ The Properties dialog box appears.

9 Click **Color** or **Black and White** (○ changes to ◉).

10 Select other properties specific to your brand of printer.

Note: The Properties dialog box may vary depending on the printer you have installed.

11 Click **OK**.

12 Click **OK** in the Page Setup and Print dialog boxes.

■ The image prints.

PRINT AN IMAGE FROM A MAC

You can print your
Photoshop Elements
image from a Mac to
create a hard copy of
your work.

PRINT AN IMAGE FROM A MAC

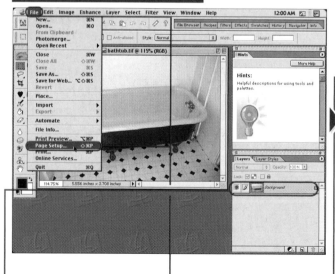

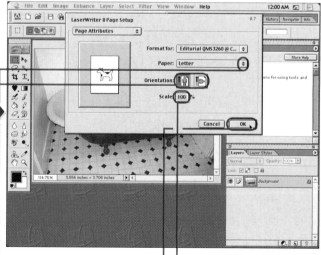

SET UP THE PAGE

1 Make sure that the layers
you want to print are visible.

*Note: An 👁 means that a layer is
visible. To learn more about layers,
see Chapter 8.*

2 Click **File**.

3 Click **Page Setup**.

■ The Page Setup dialog
box appears.

4 Click ⬍ and click a
paper type.

5 Click an orientation
button (▯) or (▭).

■ You can type a value to
increase or decrease the
size of your image on the
page.

6 Click **OK**.

■ Your page options are set.

What is halftoning?

In grayscale printing, halftoning is the process by which a printer creates the appearance of different shades of gray using only black ink. If you look closely at a grayscale image that you have printed on most black-and-white laser printers, you will see that the image consists of tiny, differently sized dot patterns. Larger dots produce the darker gray areas of the image while smaller dots produce the lighter gray areas. To apply halftoning, click **Image, Mode,** and then **Bitmap.** In the Bitmap dialog box, you can type an output value. You can also select a halftone pattern by clicking ▼ (◆) in the Method box.

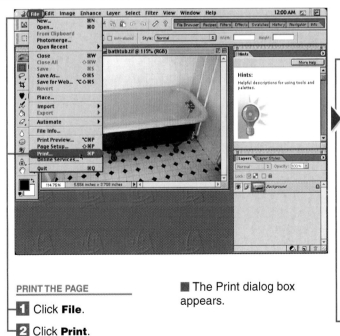

PRINT THE PAGE

1 Click **File**.

2 Click **Print**.

■ The Print dialog box appears.

3 Click ◆ and click a printer.

4 Type the number of copies you want.

5 Click a range of pages you want to print (○ changes to ◉) and type a range, if necessary.

6 Click **Print**.

■ The image prints.

PREVIEW A PRINTOUT

Elements lets you preview your printout, as well as adjust the size and positioning of your printed image, in the Print Preview dialog box. Previewing allows you to check your work without having to actually print on paper.

PREVIEW A PRINTOUT

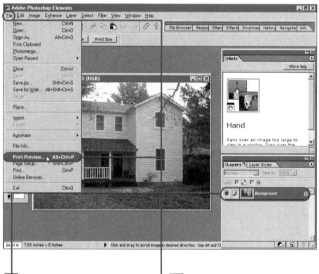

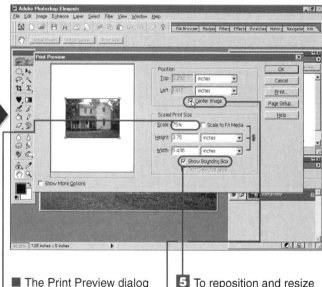

1 Make sure that the layers you want to print are visible.

Note: An ☀ means that a layer is visible. To learn more about layers, see Chapter 8.

2 Click **File**.

3 Click **Print Preview**.

■ The Print Preview dialog box appears.

4 Type a percentage in the Scale box to shrink or enlarge the image.

5 To reposition and resize the image, click **Show Bounding Box** (☐ changes to ☑).

6 Click **Center Image** to allow for the repositioning of the image (☑ changes to ☐).

286

How can I maximize the size of my image on the printed page?

In the Print Preview dialog box, you can click **Scale to Fit Media** (☐ changes to ☑) to scale the image to the maximum size for the current printing settings.

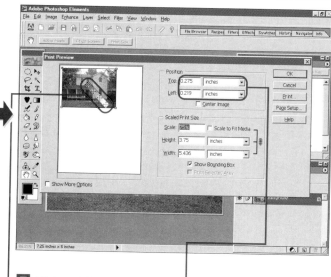

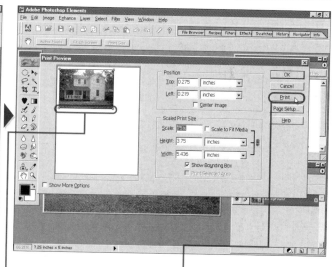

7 Click and drag in the image window to reposition the image on the page.

■ You can position your image precisely by typing values in the Top and Left fields.

■ Handles on the image edges enable you to scale the image by clicking and dragging.

8 Click **OK** to exit the Print Preview dialog box.

■ To print the image, you can click **Print**.

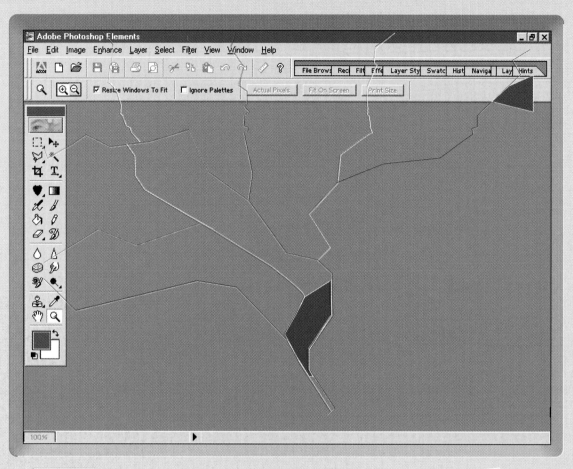

CHAPTER 15

Performance Tips

Photoshop Elements is notorious for using up lots of computer memory. This chapter gives you some tips on making sure that the application has enough memory to run at top speed. It also shows you how to ensure that Elements uses what memory it is given efficiently.

ALLOCATE SCRATCH DISK SPACE

You can give Elements extra memory — known as *scratch disk space* — from your hard drive to use when it runs out of RAM, or random access memory. This enables you to open up more files at once.

ALLOCATE SCRATCH DISK SPACE

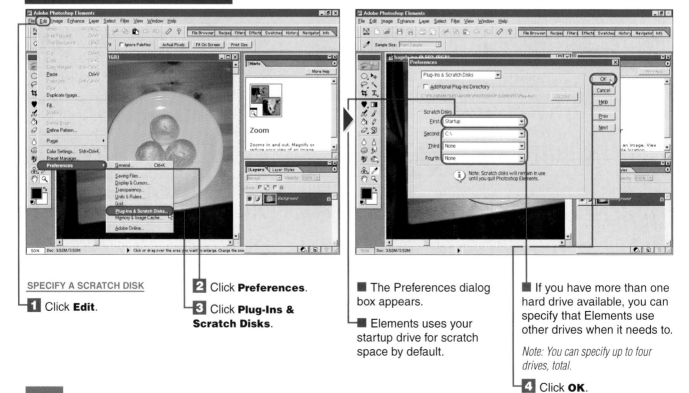

SPECIFY A SCRATCH DISK

1 Click **Edit**.

2 Click **Preferences**.

3 Click **Plug-Ins & Scratch Disks**.

■ The Preferences dialog box appears.

■ Elements uses your startup drive for scratch space by default.

■ If you have more than one hard drive available, you can specify that Elements use other drives when it needs to.

Note: You can specify up to four drives, total.

4 Click **OK**.

How do I allocate more RAM to Elements?

On a PC, click **Edit**, **Preferences**, and then **Memory & Image Cache**. To boost the RAM allocated to Elements, increase the Used by Photoshop value. On a Macintosh, you can select the Elements application icon in the Finder, and then click **File**, **Get Info**, and **Memory**. You can set the minimum and preferred memory sizes in the Adobe Photoshop Info dialog box that appears.

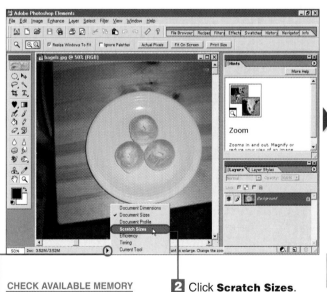

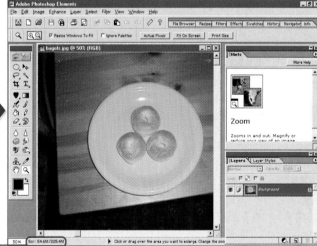

CHECK AVAILABLE MEMORY

1 Click ▶.

2 Click **Scratch Sizes**.

■ The left number is the amount of memory being used by Elements. The right number is the total amount of RAM available.

Note: If the left number is greater than the right, Elements is using scratch disk space.

USING THE PURGE COMMAND

You can free up the RAM that Elements uses to remember past commands so that it can use this memory for other purposes. This can boost Elements' speed.

USING THE PURGE COMMAND

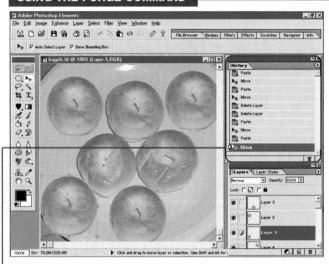

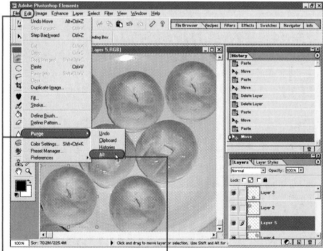

■ Elements displays previously executed commands in the History palette. Each command represents information stored in your computer's memory.

■ If the History palette is hidden, you can click **Window** and then **Show History** to display it.

-1 Click **Edit**.

-2 Click **Purge**.

■ To purge the previous command, a stored cut or copy command, or History palette commands, click **Undo**, **Clipboard**, or **Histories**, respectively.

-3 To purge all the information, click **All**.

Why can freeing up memory cause Elements to run faster?

When all the available fast memory (RAM) in your computer is used up, Elements has to start storing information in your computer's hard drive memory. This memory is much slower. Consequently, purging Elements' memory and keeping as much RAM free as possible can keep the application running at top speed.

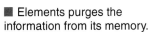

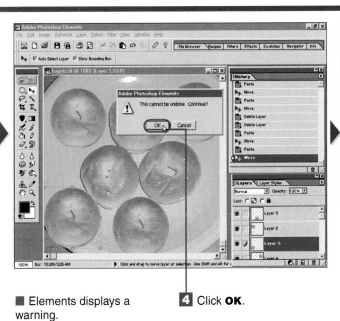

■ Elements displays a warning.

4 Click **OK**.

■ Elements purges the information from its memory.

■ Elements deletes all the commands but the most recent one from the History palette.

ADJUST HISTORY SETTINGS

You can control the amount of information stored in the History palette. This enables you to keep that information from taking up too much memory and slowing down Elements.

ADJUST HISTORY SETTINGS

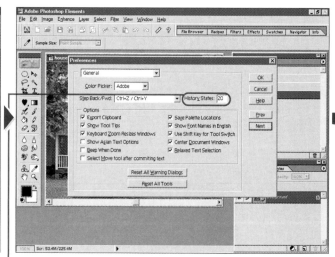

■ Elements displays previously executed commands in the History palette.

■ If the History palette is hidden, you can click **Window** and then **Show History** to display it.

1 Click **Edit**.

2 Click **Preferences**.

3 Click **General**.

■ The Preferences dialog box appears with the General preferences showing.

■ The History States value is the maximum number of commands Elements will remember at a time.

Note: To find out how to use the History palette to undo commands, see Chapter 2.

294

How much RAM, or random access memory, does Elements need to run efficiently?

When it comes to running Elements efficiently, you can never have enough RAM. Multilayered files can take up many megabytes of memory when you have them open. Elements also uses RAM for every command it stores in its history. Adobe recommends that users have at least 64MB of RAM as well as 150MB available hard drive space to run Elements, but it is a good idea to have twice that, especially if you are working with large files that have a lot of layers.

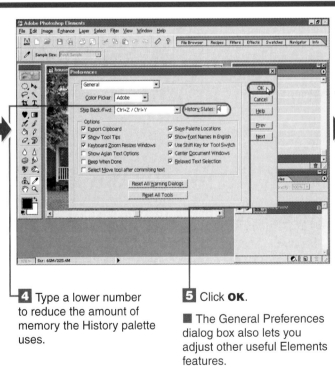

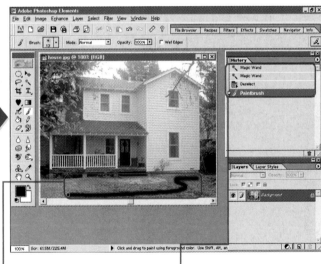

4 Type a lower number to reduce the amount of memory the History palette uses.

5 Click **OK**.

■ The General Preferences dialog box also lets you adjust other useful Elements features.

6 Perform a command.

■ In this example, the paintbrush was used.

■ Elements deletes older History commands it had previously saved.

INDEX

INDEX

horizontal type, add to an image, 230–231
hue, adjust, 132–133
Hue/Saturation command, 132–133

I

illustrations, save as GIF, 270–271
image compression, defined, 269
image files
    convert, 248–249
    rename, 249
    resize, 250–251
image orientation, Mac, 284
Image Size dialog box
    image resolutions, 50–51
    on-screen size adjustments, 46–47
    print size adjustments, 48–49
image sources, 11
Image Window, 10
images
    adjust size in print preview, 286
    artistic filter effects, 198–199
    automatic brightness levels, 130
    automatic contrast adjustment, 125
    backlighting adjustment, 140
    blur, 200–201
    brightness change, 124–125
    browse, 24–25
    canvas size adjustments, 52–53
    captions, 278–279
    change dimensions proportionally, 47, 49
    colored border addition, 115
    contact sheet, 252–253
    contrast change, 124–125
    convert sizes, 250–251
    correction recipes, 20–21
    create from scratch, 11
    create new, 26–27
    crop, 54–55
    cutout, 222–223
    directional blurs, 201
    distort, 204–205
    drop shadows, 182–183
    emboss, 220–221
    file placements, 28–29
    file size for Web, 273
    file storage guidelines, 25
    fit on screen adjustment methods, 37
    frame, 184–185
    ghosted white layer application, 113
    glowing edges, 212–213
    grayscale conversion, 137
    Hand tool views, 36–37
    highlight adjustment, 130–131
    horizontal type addition, 230–231
    hue adjustment, 132–133
    increase area with Crop tool, 55
    increase/decrease saturation, 136–137
    invert bright/dark colors, 127
    lens flare, 217
    make transparent, 272–273
    midtone adjustment, 130–131
    minimize GIF, 271
    minimize size, 287

noise addition, 206–207
offset, 224–225
on-screen size adjustments, 46–47
on-screen size versus print size, 47
opacity setting, 105
open existing, 22–23
open recently used, 23
panoramic, 258–261
poster look, 146
preview printed size, 49
preview printout, 286–287
print, 282–283
print resolution adjustments, 50–51
print size adjustments, 48–49
print with caption, 278
rainbow gradient addition, 121
reposition, 287
resample, 51
resolution considerations, 26
revert to previously saved state, 43
saturation adjustment, 132–133
save, 30, 264–275
save photographic, 268
scale proportionally, 83
scroll bar adjustments, 36
select all pixels, 66
shadow adjustment, 130–131
sharpen, 202–203
sharpen/blur, 128–129
snap to grid adjustments, 39
spotlight, 216–217
supported file formats, 23
supported file types, 23
texture addition, 214–215
thumbnail, 253
turn into charcoal sketch, 210–211
turn into shapes, 208–209
unreverted state, 43
upload to Web server, 256
use in other applications, 266–267
uses, 5
Web-safe colors, 274–275
Impressionist Brush, 106–107
inches, measurement units, 15
inner glows, layer addition, 193
inner shadow, add to a layer, 189
intensity, layer style, 195

J

JPEG (Joint Photographic Experts Group) file format, 11, 23, 268–269
jpg extension, JPEG format, 269

K

keyboard shortcuts, preferences, 14
keyboards, copy/paste selections, 78

L

labels, add to images, 7
laser printers, image resolution, 26

INDEX

INDEX

Visual

Read Less – Learn More™

Simply the Easiest Way to Learn

Simplified®

For visual learners who are brand-new to a topic and want to be shown, not told, how to solve a problem in a friendly, approachable way.

All *Simplified®* books feature friendly Disk characters who demonstrate and explain the purpose of each task.

Title	ISBN	Price
America Online® Simplified®, 2nd Ed.	0-7645-3433-5	$27.99
America Online® Simplified®, 3rd Ed.	0-7645-3673-7	$24.99
Computers Simplified®, 5th Ed.	0-7645-3524-2	$27.99
Creating Web Pages with HTML Simplified®, 2nd Ed.	0-7645-6067-0	$27.99
Excel 97 Simplified®	0-7645-6022-0	$27.99
Excel 2002 Simplified®	0-7645-3589-7	$27.99
FrontPage® 2000® Simplified®	0-7645-3450-5	$27.99
FrontPage® 2002® Simplified®	0-7645-3612-5	$27.99
Internet and World Wide Web Simplified®, 3rd Ed.	0-7645-3409-2	$27.99
Microsoft® Access 2000 Simplified®	0-7645-6058-1	$27.99
Microsoft® Excel 2000 Simplified®	0-7645-6053-0	$27.99
Microsoft® Office 2000 Simplified®	0-7645-6052-2	$29.99
Microsoft® Word 2000 Simplified®	0-7645-6054-9	$27.99
More Windows® 95 Simplified®	1-56884-689-4	$27.99
More Windows® 98 Simplified®	0-7645-6037-9	$27.99
Office 97 Simplified®	0-7645-6009-3	$29.99
Office XP Simplified®	0-7645-0850-4	$29.99
PC Upgrade and Repair Simplified®, 2nd Ed.	0-7645-3560-9	$27.99
Windows® 95 Simplified®	1-56884-662-2	$27.99
Windows® 98 Simplified®	0-7645-6030-1	$27.99
Windows® 2000 Professional Simplified®	0-7645-3422-X	$27.99
Windows® Me Millennium Edition Simplified®	0-7645-3494-7	$27.99
Windows® XP Simplified®	0-7645-3618-4	$27.99
Word 97 Simplified®	0-7645-6011-5	$27.99
Word 2002 Simplified®	0-7645-3588-9	$27.99

Over 10 million *Visual* books in print!

with these full-color Visual™ guides

The Fast and Easy Way to Learn

Discover how to use what you learn with "Teach Yourself" tips

Title	ISBN	Price
Teach Yourself Access 97 VISUALLY™	0-7645-6026-3	$29.99
Teach Yourself FrontPage® 2000 VISUALLY™	0-7645-3451-3	$29.99
Teach Yourself HTML VISUALLY™	0-7645-3423-8	$29.99
Teach Yourself the Internet and World Wide Web VISUALLY™, 2nd Ed.	0-7645-3410-6	$29.99
Teach Yourself Microsoft® Access 2000 VISUALLY™	0-7645-6059-X	$29.99
Teach Yourself Microsoft® Excel 97 VISUALLY™	0-7645-6063-8	$29.99
Teach Yourself Microsoft® Excel 2000 VISUALLY™	0-7645-6056-5	$29.99
Teach Yourself Microsoft® Office 2000 VISUALLY™	0-7645-6051-4	$29.99
Teach Yourself Microsoft® PowerPoint® 2000 VISUALLY™	0-7645-6060-3	$29.99
Teach Yourself More Windows® 98 VISUALLY™	0-7645-6044-1	$29.99
Teach Yourself Office 97 VISUALLY™	0-7645-6018-2	$29.99
Teach Yourself Red Hat® Linux® VISUALLY™	0-7645-3430-0	$29.99
Teach Yourself VISUALLY™ Access 2002	0-7645-3691-9	$29.99
Teach Yourself VISUALLY™ Adobe® Acrobat® 5 PDF	0-7645-3667-2	$29.99
Teach Yourself VISUALLY™ Adobe® Photoshop® Elements	0-7645-3678-8	$29.99
Teach Yourself VISUALLY™ Adobe® Premiere® 6	0-7645-3664-8	$29.99
Teach Yourself VISUALLY™ Computers, 3rd Ed.	0-7645-3525-0	$29.99
Teach Yourself VISUALLY™ Digital Photography	0-7645-3565-X	$29.99
Teach Yourself VISUALLY™ Dreamweaver® 3	0-7645-3470-X	$29.99
Teach Yourself VISUALLY™ Dreamweaver® 4	0-7645-0851-2	$29.99
Teach Yourself VISUALLY™ E-commerce with FrontPage®	0-7645-3579-X	$29.99
Teach Yourself VISUALLY™ Excel 2002	0-7645-3594-3	$29.99
Teach Yourself VISUALLY™ Fireworks® 4	0-7645-3566-8	$29.99
Teach Yourself VISUALLY™ Flash™ 5	0-7645-3540-4	$29.99
Teach Yourself VISUALLY™ FrontPage® 2002	0-7645-3590-0	$29.99
Teach Yourself VISUALLY™ Illustrator® 10	0-7645-3654-0	$29.99
Teach Yourself VISUALLY™ iMac™	0-7645-3453-X	$29.99
Teach Yourself VISUALLY™ Investing Online	0-7645-3459-9	$29.99
Teach Yourself VISUALLY™ Macromedia® Web Collection	0-7645-3648-6	$39.99
Teach Yourself VISUALLY™ Networking, 2nd Ed.	0-7645-3534-X	$29.99
Teach Yourself VISUALLY™ Office XP	0-7645-0854-7	$29.99
Teach Yourself VISUALLY™ Photoshop® 6	0-7645-3513-7	$29.99
Teach Yourself VISUALLY™ PowerPoint® 2002	0-7645-3660-5	$29.99
Teach Yourself VISUALLY™ Windows® 2000 Server	0-7645-3428-9	$29.99
Teach Yourself VISUALLY™ Windows® Me Millennium Edition	0-7645-3495-5	$29.99
Teach Yourself VISUALLY™ Windows® XP	0-7645-3619-2	$29.99
Teach Yourself VISUALLY™ Word 2002	0-7645-3587-0	$29.99
Teach Yourself Windows® 95 VISUALLY™	0-7645-6001-8	$29.99
Teach Yourself Windows® 98 VISUALLY™	0-7645-6025-5	$29.99
Teach Yourself Windows® 2000 Professional VISUALLY™	0-7645-6040-9	$29.99
Teach Yourself Word 97 VISUALLY™	0-7645-6032-8	$29.99

For visual learners who want to guide themselves through the basics of any technology topic. *Teach Yourself VISUALLY* offers more expanded coverage than our bestselling *Simplified* series.

The **Visual**™ series is available wherever books are sold, or call **1-800-762-2974.** Outside the US, call **317-572-3993**

ORDER FORM

TRADE & INDIVIDUAL ORDERS

Phone: **(800) 762-2974**
or **(317) 572-3993**
FAX : **(800) 550-2747**
or **(317) 572-4002**

EDUCATIONAL ORDERS & DISCOUNTS

Phone: **(800) 434-2086**
FAX : **(317) 572-4005**

CORPORATE ORDERS FOR VISUAL™ SERIES

Phone: **(800) 469-6616**
FAX : **(905) 890-9434**

Qty	ISBN	Title	Price	Total

Shipping & Handling Charges

	Description	First book	Each add'l. book	Total
Domestic	Normal	$4.50	$1.50	$
	Two Day Air	$8.50	$2.50	$
	Overnight	$18.00	$3.00	$
International	Surface	$8.00	$8.00	$
	Airmail	$16.00	$16.00	$
	DHL Air	$17.00	$17.00	$

Subtotal _____

CA residents add
applicable sales tax _____

IN, MA and MD
residents add
5% sales tax _____

IL residents add
6.25% sales tax _____

RI residents add
7% sales tax _____

TX residents add
8.25% sales tax _____

Shipping _____

Total _____

Ship to:

Name _____

Address _____

Company _____

City/State/Zip _____

Daytime Phone _____

Payment: □ Check to Hungry Minds (US Funds Only)
□ Visa □ Mastercard □ American Express

Card # _____ Exp. _____ Signature _____

Hungry Minds™

*maran*Graphics®